The Manhattan Psalter

The Manhattan Psalter

The Lectio Divina of Sister Juanita Colón

M. Juanita Colón, o.c.s.o.

THE LITURGICAL PRESS
Collegeville, Minnesota

www.litpress.org

Contents

Introduction

My first memory of Juanita Colon is a vivid one. She was the gloomiest postulant I ever encountered! At the time, we had a dairy herd of Holsteins, selling the milk to a dairy as a means of self-support for our community. I was in charge of the morning barn work, and Juanita (who had just been given the name Sister Marietta) was sent to work on my crew. It was right before Christmas, and there was a little Christmas decorating to do in the barn—yes, even in the cow barn—because life in a monastery is life with a clear focus on living with the liturgy. Nothing should be left out of the celebration, even if it can't share consciously as we humans do. I asked Sister Marietta to decorate a corner or two. She looked even more morose at the prospect, but she did it. To my surprise, she was still with us the next day, which grew into weeks and months and years. Her perseverance, however, was not gloomy. It was not long before her lively sense of humor became apparent, and her talent for cartoons suraced. But there was a lot more to Sister Marietta than cartoons!

Many years later, when I knew Juanita's story, I realized why she had been so gloomy that first week she was at Mt. St. Mary's. She had come from New York City, the big bustling city full of people, full of noise, lights, drama, and culture. She had come from being a highly trained seamstress and behind the scenes clothes designer for an exclusive shop on 5th Avenue. She was feminine and fun, she was cultured in her tastes, finding ways to attend the opera among the standing only patrons, reading Charles Dickens with a lifelong passion. She was a "Latin from Manhattan" with a passion for the city, and she found herself in what must have seemed to her hillbilly country, facing nature in the raw. No wonder her soul grew immediate icicles as she faced a dreary future with odorous barns and very large animals. She was *not* an "animal person"!

One of the factors that enabled Sister Marietta to survive the culture shock, and other facets of monastic life that grated on her sensitivities, was the abbess under whom she was to live most of her monastic life. Mother Angela Norton was also a New Yorker, also talented in music, wit, drama, and writing. She understood the postulant's loneliness and disorientation, and she understood her soul, as far as anybody can understand the mystery that is the soul of another. Sister Marietta loved this woman who led with genuine devotion. She came to love the community too. The years went by, and the postulant became a novice, then made profession of first vows and finally vows for life. She was part of a good sized group, the members of which both supported and tried the spirits of one another.

There is no such thing as the monastic nun type, so there was and still is a great variety of characters in the monastery. She had a number of opposites within her own character: lively and outgoing, even flamboyant, but also extremely private; a free spirit but also very traditional; often smouldering under a serene exterior, with a heart and snapping black eyes that could flame with love or with anger. Sister Marietta had entered as a Lay Sister. These sisters worked longer hours than the Choir Sisters, enabling the latter to spend the long hours in choir known as the "Work of God." The great bulk of this "Work of God" is the singing of psalms. After Vatican II, a decree of unification was promulgated, and all of the Lay Brothers and Sisters in the monasteries of the Cistercians of the Strict Observance were given the same status as the Choir, though they did not have to attend choir if they preferred the shorter, simpler Office they already had. Sister Marietta eagerly joined the choir where her lovely voice was a welcome addition.

After Mother Angela's death in 1986, I came to know Sister Marietta in a new way. I had always appreciated her but had not known her personal story. She asked to resume her baptismal name, and so became Sister Juanita. She served the community in various capacities besides the skilled sewing and regular community work she had always done. She was prioress for a while, then briefly "cellarer," appearing uncharacteristically with a hammer in her hand and a screwdriver sticking out of her pocket. Then she went to Rome to serve in the Generalate of our order as a secretary for two years. Toward the end of this time, she returned home with some health concerns. She was asked to attend the General Chapter to do secretarial work, and it was in Rome again for the Chapter that the results of some tests she had undergone came in positive for multiple myeloma, the disease that eventually took her life. Returning home after the Chapter, she became the abbey secretary as well as my personal secretary. She put on a bold front as she battled with the disease. Three years later she valiantly served at a second General Chapter, returning home to continue with life as usual, concealing her failing health as long as possible. She collapsed on Easter 1999 and died on August 9.

Sister Juanita began writing the psalms in her own words in the late spring of 1982. She was working on typing the fifth and final draft in the Infirmary a week before she died. The psalms reflect the reality of Israel's relationship with God. They were Jesus' prayers as a good Jew, and they are the heritage of both Jews and Christians. Sister Juanita entered into them in the same honest way, not withholding from God any of her humanity. As a contemplative nun she prayed them for all people on earth in all their various situations. She also prayed them for her own interior battles with the forces within herself. That is why her version of the Psalter is so very alive.

When a sister dies in the monastery, her body is received into the church, and her sisters keep watch with her from that moment and through the night until her funeral Mass and burial in our cemetery. During the watch, the Psalter is recited by pairs of sisters in turn, alternating with times of silent prayer. The community was not aware of Sister Juanita's "Manhattan Psalter" until that time, when it was made available in manuscript form for her wake. It was indeed a striking farewell to our sister, who had so loved life, as she entered into eternal life.

Mother M. Agnes Day, O.C.S.O.
Abbess, Mt. St. Mary's Abbey
Wrentham, Massachusetts
February 11, 2002

BOOK I

Psalms 1-41

psalm 1

WHAT A WONDERFUL LIFE THEY LEAD, those who don't follow bad example, who don't go around with sinners and scoff at holy things. But who delight in doing God's will, who think about his laws day and night and about ways to follow him more closely.

They're like trees that grow along riverbanks, heavy with luscious fruit season after season, their leaves always green. Everything they do turns out right.

But sinners—that's a different story. They're as unstable as dust blown around by any breeze. *That* for them on Judgment Day! There'll be no room for them among the just and upright.

How closely God watches over his friends—but his enemies will get what's coming to them!

psalm

2

HOW FOOLISH PEOPLE ARE to rage against God. How strange that they should think they can pit themselves against the Almighty. Their rulers and leaders rebel; they put their heads together to devise foolish plots against the Lord and against his chosen one. "Come on," they hiss, "let's shake off these chains and free ourselves from this degrading servitude!"

But God just laughs at them—how ludicrous, how ridiculous they are. Then, in sudden anger he wheels on them when they least expect it, paralyzing them with fear. "This is my chosen one," he thunders, "I myself have installed him as king over Jerusalem, my own holy city."

And the king for his part says: "Yes, listen carefully to what he says, for he swore to me, 'You're my son from this day on and forever, and I'm your Father. Ask me for anything you want and it's yours. The nations, the earth, everything is yours. Rule over it all with an iron hand—crush it if necessary. I put it all into your power.'"

You rulers and leaders of the earth, have you heard? Pay attention while there's still time. Bow your proud heads, serve the Lord, kiss his feet in awe and trembling, or else—you know his anger. It can burst into consuming fire in an instant.

Happy are those who cultivate God's friendship.

O H, HOW THEY HATE ME, not a friend in sight! All they do is talk about me, saying, "Hey! Here's our chance; God's turned against him. He's fallen right into our hands!"

But they're wrong, Lord. Aren't they? You're still on my side, standing up for me, fighting my battles, cheering me up when I'm low.

Yes, whenever I pray to him, he always answers. Why, at night I drop off to sleep as trustingly as a child, and I awake, refreshed, ready to face a new day because he's watched over me through the night. So let them come at me, let them do their worst. I stand ready to face a thousand of them if I have to.

Come on, Lord, be my defense, shut their lying mouths and break their power. You alone have the answer to life's sorrows. May your blessing come down upon all of us.

4

LORD, WHENEVER I'VE NEEDED YOU, you've always been there. Be with me now again, as I pour out my griefs and present my case.

Listen to me, all of you with power, how long do you think I'm going to put up with your contemptuous insults? How long are you going to waste time and energy on a hopeless cause? Understand, once and for all, that God's admitted me into his intimate friendship and I have his ear whenever I want it. Fear God, fear him I say, and then you'll see the light. Think. Think hard as you lie on your beds in the still of the night, and then come—admit defeat and join the worshiping crowd. Cast your lot with the Lord!

So many sigh in these times, Lord, "Oh, if only things would go better for us. . . ." Lord, let them feel the warmth of your love as I have. Why, the joy of loving you far surpasses anything the world has to offer. At night, as soon as I close my eyes, I drop right off to sleep, secure in the knowledge of your love, and I have the comfort of knowing that under your loving gaze I'm perfectly safe from harm.

O LORD, PLEASE LISTEN to what I'm trying to say. Don't my sighs
mean anything to you? I tell you I need you, my king and my
God! Every morning, bathed in the light of the rising sun, I start my
day with prayer, laying all my needs before you, confidently expect-
ing your mercy.

How pure and all-holy you are, how hateful sin is to you. You
allow nothing unclean to approach you. Just the sight of evildoers is
an abomination to you; you recoil in disgust and annihilate them.
Truly they are a blot on the landscape, these liars, these violent, these
vengeful people.

But you allow me to enter your holy place. Oh, what mercy, what
love! You accept my worship. Mine. I prostrate myself before you,
trembling and weeping for joy. And I'm hated for it, Lord. Yes, I've
made powerful enemies on your account because of my determina-
tion to do your will, no matter what. Help me, give me the strength
to continue in loyalty and obedience. Show me the best way to remain
unshaken. They don't know what truth is! They're evil through and
through. Masters of honeyed speech, yes, but from their gaping
mouths comes the stench of an open grave.

Lord, give it to them! Sabotage all their plans, their treacherous
schemes. Let everything they plan for the downfall of others recoil
on them instead. The truth of the matter is that you're the real target
in all of this, can't you see? Once they're beaten, we, your true friends,
will have cause to rejoice again. Because we'll know that you're always
there, watching over those who really love you. What cause for continual celebration this is.

Obedience brings down blessings upon us, and nothing they do
can ever touch us.

6

GOD, PLEASE DON'T BE ANGRY with me anymore, please don't make me pay so heavily for my sins. I'm just wasting away, Lord, for this sickness has penetrated to my very bones. I'm worn out, sick, alone, afraid . . . when will it all end? Help me, O my God, give me another chance or it's the end for me.

Can the dead praise you? What glory can you receive from a corpse? I spend sleepless nights weeping, soaking the pillow with my tears. My eyes are swollen almost shut; I squint and blink like some-one old and doddering as my enemies cackle and gloat over me.

Get away from me, all of you! God's still on my side, I tell you! He hasn't turned a deaf ear to my pleading—no—he'll soon be here with all the help I need. Then all those who thirsted for my blood will find the tables turned on them—oh yes—and they'll find them-selves covered with confusion and utterly disgraced.

7

L ORD, I NEED YOU NOW as never before. Look! My enemies are in hot pursuit. Save me, or they'll tear me limb from limb like a hungry lion.

Why is this happening to me? What have I done? If I'd betrayed a friend or taken unfair advantage of my enemy (why, I had one in my clutches and let him go), then I wouldn't deserve to live. You'd be fully justified in handing me over to suffer not only death but everlasting disgrace.

But I'm innocent, Lord and you know it. Stand up for me, let them see your righteous anger in all its fury. Drag them before the public and judge them without mercy, but exonerate me before the world. Weigh these false charges against my honesty and integrity and you'll have only one choice—complete acquittal.

When, when are the evil going to get what they've got coming to them? How I long to see the victory of goodness and decency over the darkness of sin. How I long to see the upright covered with honors by the God who sees into the secrets of the heart and repays accordingly. I trust him completely because I know that ultimately he's always on the side of the right-living. But I know, too, that he's also just and no wrongdoing escapes his penetrating gaze. When sinners won't repent, God knows how to bring them to their knees. Death itself, sharp and bitter, is the final, irrevocable sentence.

The evil are utterly bloated with malice, they belch forth lies and treachery. But how they fall headlong into their own traps, their snares laid so cunningly for others. The sight makes my heart swell with gratitude toward the God who champions the innocent and helpless. All I can do is burst into song, praising my God to the skies.

psalm 8

O LORD, LORD, THE GLORY OF YOUR NAME encircles the earth and is the talk of the angels. Even children and babies prattle happily about you, to the consternation of your detractors, who are struck dumb with rage and frustration.

When I gaze up at the heavens, the glittering galaxies scattered far by your hand, the comparative nothingness of humanity staggers me.

What is it you see in human beings? How can you even give them a thought? And yet, only angels have claim to a higher place in the order of your creation. You have showered humanity with incredible honors and glory. Actually putting them in charge of your whole world, everything that lives and breathes, all of it, theirs.

O Lord, Lord, the glory of your name is the glory of the earth.

9

D EAR GOD, HOW BRIMFUL WITH GRATITUDE is my heart, how full of your praises. I must tell all the world how wonderful you are and boast of all your marvels. Oh, the joy, the exultation of it! My happiness ever flows in a bubbling litany of praise to you, Most High God.

Look at how my enemies turn tail when you come into view; they keel over like tenpins, knowing that you've acquitted me. Yes, you've passed down a favorable judgment on me from your glorious throne on high. But all who do evil, man or woman, have been condemned to oblivion. You demons, extermination is your fate, you and all your fine cities and towns with you. Who will ever even bother to think of you anymore after this?

As for my God, his reign is everlasting—and his strict justice; while everyone is assured of a fair hearing, he sees to it that the punishment fits each crime. The downtrodden and oppressed find a true champion in him, a strong protector when troubles loom. O Lord, to know you is to love you because you never turn a deaf ear in time of trouble.

Sing out his praises, all of you, shout it out for all to hear, tell everyone in sight what he's done for you. Not one tear escapes him, not one cry of distress, nor does he fail to punish those who make the innocent suffer. "Be kind to me, Lord," they cry, "Look at what I'm made to endure at the hands of my enemies. Be kind, you who have the power to snatch me back from death. Then, oh then, what tales of wonder I'll have to tell, what an outpouring of joyful praise."

See, the godless always fall into their own traps; their murderous designs are their own undoing. This is an infallible sign of God's power, and this is all that those who dare to contend with him can expect—swift judgment and the fiery pit. Because of this the poor need not fear the future, nor see their hopes drowned in despair. Come Lord, show your might. Condemn the impious and send them away in chains. Let them feel the full effects of your omnipotence.

LORD! WHERE ARE YOU? We're in desperate straits and you're nowhere in sight. Is it possible that you're unaware of how the poor are being preyed upon by the unscrupulous? They fall, all unsuspecting, into the diabolical traps set out for them, and their tormentors, swollen with pride, boast about their conquests. The ringleader, shouting defiance to the skies, says, "God? He hasn't any power over me! Why, he doesn't even exist as far as I'm concerned!" What thoughts! What blasphemy!

And the worst of it is everything the wicked do seems to succeed. They're totally devoid of the fear of God, and if any have the temerity to stand up to them, they make short work of them. "No one can beat me," they crow; "I hold all the cards!" All they know is lying, all they do is curse, all they live for is the ruination of others. They'll bide their time, waiting for their chance, then suddenly leap for your throat. The helpless and the weak are easy prey for them, of course; they specialize in the blood of the innocent. Cackling over them they hiss, "That God of yours must be sound asleep or hard of hearing, huh? He doesn't care *that* for you!"

O God, no; come to our rescue, show your love for the downtrodden. How can you allow them to say such things, to believe that there's no retribution? But you do see, I know it; you do hear, I can swear to it. You are there, with all the love and power at your command to come to the aid of those in need, those who have no one but you.

Break the stranglehold of the wicked; don't let one crime go unpunished. You're king, and they're nothing; soon to vanish without a trace. Humble supplication has been heard: you've supplied the strength to endure trial and persecution—upholding the rights of the fatherless and dispossessed so that the future may hold no more terrors for them.

G OD IS MY REFUGE in all my troubles, so why all these warnings
of "Flee, flee . . . "? They warn me over and over again that
traps have been laid for me, and ambushes set up to waylay the innocent and unsuspecting. "What can anyone do," they groan, "when
the entire social structure of a country is rotten? Nothing but crime
and corruption everywhere!"

But God knows, I tell you. God sees; nothing escapes his all-
seeing eye. Oh, he might put his friends to the test for a time, but
what he does to his enemies is beyond imagining. He unleashes all
the forces of nature against them, lightning, earthquakes, with howling winds to buffet them from all sides. For he is just and loves justice.
That is why only the upright can expect to behold him face to face.

O GOD, HELP ME! There isn't anyone honest left, no one capable of telling the truth. Lies! Lies! That's all I hear. They lie to each other and about each other, all the while smiling sweetly. It's sickening. May God make them eat their lying words, may their calumnies stick in their throats—those who dare to say, "No one can stop us, we're invincible, complete masters of the spoken word!"

But just listen to what God says: "You've abused the poor and terrorized the innocent. Now I'm going to show you who's master here! I'll deprive you of your victims and surround them with my powerful protection."

You can depend on his word. It's like the purest and finest silver, fresh from the crucible. O Lord, I know you'll keep your promises and stand between us and this corrupt generation. The entire social structure is sick because of the crime in high places. And criminals are treated like conquering heroes.

13

L ORD, HOW LONG are you going to ignore me? How long are you
going to keep that unyielding back turned to me? Forever?
How much longer must I struggle on, without light, without a shred
of consolation? You're breaking my heart! How long are you going to
let my enemies lord it over me? Please answer me.

Dear God, won't you put the sparkle of life back into my eyes? I
feel the very soul draining out of me. How happy my persecutors
would be, what a triumph for them to see me done for. How they
would crow, "You see? We've won! He's finished!"

But no, I trust in you, O Lord, in spite of how things look for me,
in spite of all the evidence to the contrary. Happiness is in store for
me, it'll all come back once you've relented and helped me. Come,
Lord, I'm longing to say again, "This God of mine really loves me!"

ONLY ASSES WOULD GO AROUND muttering to themselves, "God?—what God?—there's no God—nonsense!" Oh, people today are so corrupt, their conduct so reprehensible it seems as if there isn't an honest one left anywhere.

And God? He's up there scanning the earth, looking for at least one who cares enough about salvation to worry about it. But no, they're all the same. No one cares, not one. This life is all they think about.

God sighs, "When, when are they going to see the light? Look at them, spending all their time going from bad to worse, fattening themselves on the helpless, victimizing the innocent. Prayer? The thought never enters their heads!"

But wait, sudden nameless fears will invade their worldly hearts. They'll discover, to their dismay, that God is always on the side of the underdog.

Yes, you demons, you may laugh callously as you make the poor beg for mercy, but God will pluck them safely out of your clutches and then—*that* for you!

Then, and may it be soon, what joy, what mad joy! What wild rejoicing for Jacob, what floods of happy tears in Israel.

L ORD, PLEASE TELL ME. What does someone have to do to get into
your inner circle?

"My real friends are right-living, obedient, and sincere.

"They don't gossip about others, recklessly destroying good names
and reputations.

"They're loyal and don't hold grudges, but willingly and generously
forgive wrongs.

"They don't go around with irreverent scoffers but are always the
first to show respect for God's friends.

"They honor their word even if it could mean financial ruin.

"They never get rich by extorting money.

"They can't be bought or made to commit perjury.

"All of these can count on my assistance in time of trial. Nothing
can ever shake them."

TAKE CARE OF ME, LORD, PLEASE. You know how I rely on you. My constant refrain is, "Lord, Lord, you are my all."

How I love the holy ones of this world, the saints—these are the real people, God's masterpieces. But idol-worshipers? They've only themselves to blame for their griefs. Share in their filthy practices? Not me. I wouldn't soil my lips with the names of their pagan deities. No, it's you I want, O God, you alone in all the world—why, my life is in your hands. With God looking after me, life is one vast sunlit meadow. I bless and praise him for he's always at my side, guiding me, advising me at every step. I'm deeply attentive to his voice within me. With such a counselor what could ever go wrong? I'm so happy, bursting with a sense of well-being.

I feel, Lord, that my soul won't have to wander aimlessly among the dead in the underworld, that I won't suffer the corruption of the grave. You've shown me the right way to live, helped me to understand the joy of loving you, made me understand that it's in your power to grant everlasting life.

L ORD, I DEMAND A HEARING! How is it possible that my shrieks of distress don't reach you? I'm innocent, I tell you, innocent. You must, in all justice, acquit me, and in front of everyone. You've put me to the test many times, tried me with dreadful nightmares. Have I failed the test? Never. I've never entertained a thought that I'd be ashamed to put into words. I've refused to follow the crowd, and by adhering strictly to your commandments I've managed to avoid pitfall after pitfall. Yes, the straight and narrow path. Always.

You see now why I don't hesitate to plead with you; I've no reason to fear rebuff. My conscience is clear. Won't you please listen to me? Let me see that marvelous kindness of yours at work again. No one can resist you once you take someone's part against the enemy. Be good to me, Lord, protect me, Lord, as you would a favorite. How they hate me. How they watch for their chance to finish me. They've closed their hearts to me and covered me with insults, boasting of their superiority. Lions on the prowl couldn't be craftier or more treacherous.

Lord, send them sprawling, knock them into the dirt, fill them with such wild panic that they run into each other in complete confusion! O God, deliver me from these coarse and worldly enemies who think of nothing but gratifying their appetites and ambitions. They pile up great stores of riches which they leave to their children, thus perpetuating their follies from generation to generation.

I don't envy them, I have my dream—I long for the joy of divine communion, which will be satisfied when I at last behold your face.

I LOVE YOU, I LOVE YOU, LORD! You fill me with strength and well-being. The Lord is like a great walled fortress, he is the foundation of my life, my Savior. How else can I describe him? He is like a mighty mountain top, unscalable, an impregnable stronghold where I am shielded from attack. I have only to call upon God, all-worthy of praise, and I am saved from my enemies.

I thought I was finished for good this time. Death, cold and cruel, was staring me in the face. I was being tossed about on an ocean of troubles, being dragged helplessly down, down into the depths. I screamed and screamed, "O God, help me!"

And he heard. My shrieks reached his ear and he sprang into action. The earth shook as if in the throes of a violent earthquake. So great was his rage that it seemed as if flames were shooting from his nostrils. The heavens themselves were ablaze. Then down he came, everything in creation bending before his blast as he strode masterfully, black clouds under his feet. He leaped astride a cherub and streaked across the skies with the speed of the wind, wrapping himself in a cloak of thunderclouds, a wall of dense mist moving before him, veiling his approach.

Then suddenly the darkness flew apart, and in a blaze of light, there he stood, a light was so intense and searing that even stones burst into flame. And his voice—a great roar filled the air, an ear-splitting blast of sound burst from the mighty God, accompanied by hailstones and blinding flashes of lightning. The very seas shrank back in terror and the ocean bed was revealed—one saw with the naked eye the foundations of the earth. All this merely from the air shuddering before his anger, the sheer force of his fury sweeping everything before it.

Suddenly I felt his strong arms close about me, lifting me, plucking me, still screaming, from the surging flood waters. I was safe— oh, the joy of it! Safe from my would-be murderers. From those who were too many for me. They had assaulted me, hit me when I was down, but they hadn't reckoned with the Lord. He came to my rescue, set me free because he loves me—he loves me.

I've been true to him, so he's been true to me. I resisted temptation, my hands were clean; he knew it and rewarded me magnificently. How just and fair he is. Yes, I've always tried to be a loyal steadfast friend to my God. "Count on me!" I'd cry, and I've backed up my words with a strict adherence to his laws. I've never deliberately done my own will, but kept careful watch on myself lest I be surprised into a slip of any kind. And he, just like a true and loyal friend to me (and how much more so), rained down blessings on me, so satisfied was he with my poor efforts.

O my God, you really are a true friend to those who are true to you, open and fair with all who are open and fair with you, but to the devious and hypocritical you give lessons in sharp-dealing. You reward humility handsomely, but you're ruthless toward pride.

Truly, you are like a sudden brightness in a dark room, dispelling ominous shadows like a warm cheery lamp, giving one new heart. With you on my side I dare anything. Let them do their worst, come at me from every side. No barricade would be too high for me to scale. No, not for me, Lord.

In our God there is no shadow of wrong, his word is his bond. If any hide in him, he stands between them and menacing danger like a mighty shield, deflecting every attack. After all, is there any other god even worthy of the name? My God constantly pours fresh strength into me and directs my every step. I run like a deer, climb like a goat over the mountainsides, surefooted, daring. He fills me with insight and gives me the strength of ten. O Lord, you yourself have become my defender.

Your own right hand is over mine, guiding it, supporting me in every endeavor. It seems as if you've come down to my level in order to lift me to yours. A wide path opened out before me and I strode along, surefooted, purposeful.

Then—how I chased them! How they ran! It was marvelous! They were no match for me; I caught them easily and finished them off, every single one—not one survived. It was the strength you gave me, Lord, all your doing. From the beginning they were marked, for you knew very well who they were who hated me and plotted against my life. Yet, when their own false gods failed to save them, they had the temerity to cry out to the God of Israel. But he turned a deaf ear to their yowling and they fell into my waiting hands. I wiped my feet on them.

Oh God, you have delivered us from the horrors of civil war and put all the nations about us into my power. Complete strangers swore allegiance to me, entire nations groveled at my feet after they had staggered out of their ruined fortresses, weak-kneed with fear, white flags fluttering.

Our God lives! Blessed be God, my rock. Praise him—praise the Lord! He gave me victory over my persecutors, authority over other nations, and protection from those who were plotting to depose me.

I owe you everything, Lord. I'll shout your praises from the housetops; I'll fling my song of praise to the four winds so that all the world hears of it with wonder. You have kept faith with your king, honored your word, and showered blessings down upon him. Not only on David, but through him to all his lineage forever.

THE GLORY OF GOD IS BLAZONED across the heavens, everything shouts his name.

Days pass on the glad tidings to one another, nights take it up and fling it joyously one to the next. Though not a word is uttered, not a sound reaches us, yet the silence of the heavens is thunderous with praise. A jubilant message encircles the earth like a golden ring.

The sun leaps eagerly from its heavenly tent, as exultant as a bridegroom on his honeymoon, or like an athlete proudly flexing his muscles for a test of strength. It burns its way across the sky from horizon to horizon and everything feels its sting. No use trying to hide.

God's laws are so good, so absolutely perfect that just the thought of them is an inspiration. His word is so clear that even a simpleton like me can understand. What a joy to keep to his ways; he's never wrong. Everything as clear as crystal. He can never be loved too much —he's always fresh and new. Gold? Bah! His laws are a million times more precious than all the gold in the world—and sweeter to the taste than honey sucked straight from the comb. His precepts enrich and discipline the mind as well as the soul; to observe them is to have found the key to happiness and success.

But wait, there's one danger. Even though you're very scrupulous in keeping God's laws, conceit can be your undoing. O God, purge my soul of the seeds of pride. Don't let it eat away at my observance, undermining it and finally causing my complete downfall. Grant me the grace and protection of a humble heart, protect me from myself so that my conscience may be clear and my soul at peace. May my every thought and word be music to your ears, rising as a song of praise to you, O God my savior.

O KING, MAY THE LORD HEAR your every outcry. May the very sound of his name on your lips protect you. May he send you heavenly aid, reinforcements from on high. May he never forget your goodness, your many generous offerings and sacrifices. May he grant you even the things you don't dare ask for—those secret longings hidden in the depths of your soul—and bring all your cherished dreams to fulfillment.

Then we'll share your joy, happy for you and with you—joining in an exuberant, shouting, flag-waving celebration. May it please God to answer all your prayers.

But then, would God turn a deaf ear to the king? Never. Victory is assured, help is on the way—a dazzling display of divine power and strength is about to be unleashed. Let others trust in their armies and war-horses, but as for us, our weapon is the name of the Lord. They'll be demolished, and everyone will be astounded at the magnitude of our victory.

God save the king and be ever open to our prayers!

O LORD, HOW HAPPY YOU'VE MADE THE KING, how he exults over your great strength, over this new display of your power. You've given him everything he prayed for, answered all his heart's desires. You've showered personal honors on him, even a royal diadem. All he asked was that his life be spared, but you've given him eternal life. He has great renown, universal homage. And to crown all this, the ecstasy of your inner presence. You have his undying trust, for he knows that only through you did victory come.

O king, because of this, what enemy can withstand you? They all perish, the heat of your attack burning them to a crisp like logs in a fiery furnace—God's holy anger will devour them. You'll wipe them from the face of the earth, nothing will remain of their posterity. Though they planned your downfall so craftily, they were doomed to fail. Yes, send them away under a hail of burning arrows.

Praise and honor to you, O our God, may all acclaim your mighty power. Listen! Listen to our shouts of joyful praise!

22

O GOD, GOD, WHERE ARE YOU? Why don't you answer me? Have you so utterly abandoned me that you can't even hear my cries for help? I've been calling out to you day and night, a ceaseless torrent, and to no avail. Yet—I know you're there, I know it. You are ever the All-Holy, our God, the glory of Israel. What could ever change that? Our ancestors relied on you completely, and not without cause, for their trust was never betrayed. When they needed you, they only had to cry out and you were there in an instant. You saved them time and again from a shame and humiliation that is worse than death.

But me! You've made me feel less than human, nothing more than a worm. Everyone laughs at me, makes fun of me. I don't know if I can bear it.

They ridicule my faith in you, my trust, the very heart of me. "Yeah," they jeer, "this is what he gets for being so gullible. Well, if that God of his really cares about him, why doesn't he come to his rescue? Isn't that what a real friend would do?" It's horrible, the things they say.

Lord, please, all my life, even in the womb of my mother, I've been dependent on you—simply to keep me in existence if nothing else. When just a little child, a babe in arms, I could lisp your name. I was dedicated to you at birth, consecrated for your service. Please come, I'm in desperate straits; if you don't help me—there's no one. Look at them closing in on me, like wild bulls, their jowls wide open ready to tear me apart. I ache all over, my legs have turned to water. I'm dry-mouthed and weak, I can feel the strength draining out of me as they surround me, baying like hounds, snapping at my heels. They've fastened their fangs into my hands and feet, and there isn't a sound bone in my whole body. They stand there laughing while I writhe in agony. Having stripped the rags off my back, they haggle noisily over who gets what.

Father, please help me or I'm finished. Save me from these dogs who want to devour me, body and soul, if they can. Don't let me be eaten alive!

Yet, I can't help but feel that somehow it's alright, that somehow I'll once again have cause to sing your praises. "Listen, all of you," I'll cry, "all of you who love the Lord, all who've experienced his mercy and forgiveness like I have, praise the Lord! He's never turned a deaf ear to the cries of the poor. No, at the first sound of distress he leaps to their aid. Praise the Lord!"

Everyone will hear of it, Lord, as I boldly and joyfully make public renewal of my vows, shouting them out from the housetops. I'll invite all the outcasts to eat a sacrificial meal with me, and together we'll praise you as one voice. "Oh my dear friends," I'll say, "bless you, be happy!" The good news will flash around the world and nations will be falling over themselves in their eagerness to join forces with you, prostrating themselves in trembling adoration.

What a sovereign Lord is this, how vast his dominion—everything and everyone is in his power; the living, the dead, the proud, and the humble, all, all will swear allegiance to him. Our children and our children's children will lift one great cry of praise in his honor. Spread the news, tell everyone. Pass on the glad tidings as a precious heritage to future generations so that the account of his marvels may never die.

23

MY LORD WATCHES OVER ME as carefully as a shepherd, I have nothing to fear. I stretch out peacefully on fresh green grass; we stroll together along quiet streams. Just being with him refreshes my weary soul. He advises me on how best to please him and on ways to follow him more closely.

Even if I had to face death, I would do so with a quiet heart, secure in the knowledge of your comforting presence. A presence so real that it is like a strong staff to lean on and like a stout club of defense.

My enemies watch all this, so green with envy as I sit down to the magnificent spread prepared for me, just for me. Perfumed oils for my hair, food aplenty, and a dazzling array of choice wines, more than I could ever eat or drink.

Oh, the Lord will see to it that I always enjoy the best of everything, even a favored place in his own house to the very end of my days.

24

EVERYTHING BELONGS TO GOD, EVERYTHING! Land, sky, sea, peoples, animals, everything, because he is the creator of the world, setting it squarely on the seas, watering it with the sparkling rivers.

Realizing this, I pondered within myself, "Dare anyone approach such a God? Dare anyone seek admission to his intimate friendship?"

A little more thought and prayer and the answer came to me clearly. Only those whose hands are clean can approach him, whose consciences do not reproach them, who have never taken God's name in vain or indulged in lies.

That was it, of course. God can hold up people like this to others as a shining example, blessing them abundantly. These are the ones who have enough sense to understand what true happiness is, that in God, and in him alone, lies human fulfillment. Who bathe in the sunshine of your smile, O God.

Come on then, you massive gates, open up! Swing wide, you ancient doors, because the King of Glory approaches. What? Who is this King of Glory? I'll tell you who he is, he is God, Lord of the universe, strong, invincible. Come on, I say, open up, let him in! What? Can you still be asking who this is? This is God Almighty himself, I tell you, the creator of heaven and earth.

L ORD, I'M ASKING YOU, PLEASE, hear my prayers. I've always trusted you, counted on you; don't fail me now, don't give them the satisfaction of seeing me fall flat on my face. No one who trusts in you is ever betrayed; no, anyone who dares attack one of your friends has you to deal with.

O God, I do so want to understand you, but you're such a mystery. All I want is to know you better so I can follow you more closely. Please explain all this, please unravel these mysteries. You're my savior, the one I instinctively turn to in time of trouble, the one in whom I dare to hope.

Think back, Lord, on how often you've helped me in the past (I'm always in some kind of trouble!), how time and again you proved your love for me in, oh, so many ways. Won't you please overlook my badness and remember only our friendship?

How good God is. How eagerly he searches out sinners to convert them, to give them another chance. He tries to improve the law-abiding too; he delights in making the good even better, and the proficient perfect. His goodness extends to all who are loyal and true to him. (O my God, in the name of our love, tell me again that you've forgiven me, because what I did . . . was terrible, terrible . . .).

Show me the ones full of the fear of the Lord and I'll show you those God has admitted to intimate friendship. What rich and beautiful souls they have, and what an inheritance for those who come after them. Their descendants will never know the horrors of exile. God personally sees to the instruction of these, his intimates, flooding their minds with light and understanding. That's why, in all my troubles I turn to him immediately, certain of help no matter how hopeless the situation.

So now, Lord, again I'm before you, pleading my case, alone and in desperate straits. Relieve me of the anguish that's gnawing at me so I know my sins are forgiven and have peace of mind at last.

Look at how many have it in for me—how much they hate and despise me. Don't let them kill me or grind me into the ground, not after I've trusted you so. Let my fidelity and loyalty speak for me. Lord—I'm waiting . . . save me. No, save us all!

OH GOD, BACK UP MY EFFORTS to live a good life, a life anchored firmly and trustingly in you. My life's an open book; examine every part of it, put me to the test, I've nothing to fear. I've never forgotten your mercy to me, and I've tried to show my gratitude by unswerving obedience to your will.

I shun the company of liars and hypocrites, I never frequent their haunts. My hands are clean, kept scrupulously clean, so that I can enter your sanctuary with a clear conscience. . . . Everyone knows how good you've been to me; why, I've fairly shouted it from the housetops. And, oh, your temple! How I love your holy house. The processions, the hymns, the shouts of gladness. I love the very walls of the place that encloses your sacred dwelling among us.

Lord, don't include me in the punishment you've in store for malefactors, murderers, those whose greedy hands never have their fill of filthy bribes. No, I want nothing to do with them—it's you I love, your ways I follow. Don't ever let them drag me down to their level, please keep me under your protection always.

I know that in appealing to God I'm on firm ground and soon everyone will know the story, the thrilling account of my rescue.

WITH GOD LIGHTING THE WAY BEFORE ME and ever ready to catch me if I chance to stumble, what have I to fear? With him on my side, is there anyone to be afraid of? Why, when they try to do me in, they fall flat on their own faces! I feel secure enough to face an army of them—even if all hell broke loose, I'd still trust him completely.

There's only one thing I want, one thing I ask of my Lord (and intend to keep on asking) to live with him all the days of my life, to be allowed to feast my eyes on him and to drink in the beauty of his temple. To be protected within those walls, secure in the knowledge that I'm out of the reach of my enemies. There in his marble courts I can join in all the festive celebrations, leaping, singing, shouting for sheer joy.

But before that can happen—Lord, how desperate is my need. . . . Open your heart to me, answer my prayers of entreaty. My heart cried out to you, "Look at me!" I've heard your hidden prompting in the depths of my soul urging me to turn to you, and I have, truly I have. Don't be angry with me, don't turn away from me, please. You've always come to my aid in the past; don't fail me now. I've always believed that even if the unthinkable happens, my own mother and father turn against me, you'd stand by me. Repay my trust—tell me where to turn, show me how to escape from these bloodsuckers. Don't abandon me to them; they're preparing to trip me up with a lot of trumped-up charges. Liars, all of them!

What would become of me if I didn't have my hopes for salvation to lean on? I sustain myself with these thoughts, saying to myself, "Be patient—he's coming—just a little longer—you'll see."

I 'M PRAYING TO YOU, LORD. Please don't turn a deaf ear because if
you won't listen I'm finished! Oh, do listen to me. I'm calling and
calling, arms outstretched beseechingly toward your sanctuary. Don't
condemn me, don't treat me as you do those sinful hypocrites who
smile so sweetly in a person's face while all the time they're full of
curses and mockery inside.

Give it to them, Lord, give them what they deserve for their ill-
spent lives. As they've done, do to them! (Since they've shown nothing but scorn for God and his glorious creation, I know he's going to
destroy them beyond all hope of restoration.)

O praise the Lord! I feel sure my prayers have been answered,
now I know more than ever that all my strength comes from him. I
only had to trust him with all my heart and now I'm safe—he never
fails me. My heart is fairly bursting with gratitude, and I want to
sing—sing—pour out a bubbling torrent of joyful praise. See how
squarely God stands behind his people, how unfailingly he supports
his chosen leader.

Dear Lord, be with us always. May we be blessed, fed, and carried
close to your heart, forever and ever.

ACKNOWLEDGE GOD'S STRENGTH, all you heavenly beings, acknowledge his glory and awesome power. Give him the glory due his majesty; gather round him in loving reverence, worship him, glorify him by your dazzling splendor.

Listen to that mighty voice as it booms out over the waters, a sound like thunder rolling over the surging ocean. How powerful this voice; how awe-inspiring, the echo of it is enough to topple massive sequoias. Mountains quake, plunging and snorting like bull calves at its sound, bolts of lightning, a shower of fiery sparks. Vast deserts writhe and heave with excitement, and wild animals deliver their young in an exultant frenzy. This great voice alone can uproot the most gigantic trees, leveling whole forests. From his temple come exultant cries of Glory! Glory! Hallelujah!

And above this surging tumult the Lord sits enthroned, regal, majestic, everlasting. He is the One who will forever strengthen and support his people, and in the end grant them the greatest of all his gifts—everlasting peace.

O GOD, MAY YOU BE PRAISED FOREVER because once again you have come between me and almost certain disaster, not letting me become the laughingstock of my enemies. Yes, Lord, I felt already condemned to hell and extinction when you reached out, in answer to my bellowing, and pulled me back from the abyss toward which I was plunging.

Sing! Sing, you friends of God, sing songs of thanksgiving unendingly. His anger is momentary, his goodwill forever. The nights may be full of the sound of bitter weeping, but spirits soar with the morning sun. I was sitting on top of the world. I thought, "Friend, you've got it made. Relax! Enjoy life!" O Lord, you had been so good to me, so generous that it went to my head. Then, suddenly, you were gone, without a word of warning you were gone. My smile froze, my heart sank, I collapsed in a heap of self-pity. "O God!" I sobbed, "O God! What's the life of one miserable human being to you? Can a corpse give you glory? Can lips, cold and still, offer you praise? Please, Lord, mercy. Please Lord, hear me, give me another chance!"

And wonder of wonders, you answered. Just as suddenly, there you were again. My tears dried up like magic, joy and relief flooded my soul. I wanted to dance and sing with wild abandon. In an instant you stripped away the black mood I was draped in, and now I was garlanded with radiant smiles so that the jubilation that filled my soul found expression in shouts of gladness.

O God, God, let me never stop thanking you!

PROTECT ME, LORD, don't let me lose face. You know it's only right to come to the aid of the innocent. Oh, come soon, hear me! Stand between me and my enemies like a mighty mountain, like a thickly walled fortress. Yes, that's what you are to me, an unscalable height, an impregnable stronghold. Give proof, then, of your mighty power by leading me out of this maze of miseries, guiding me safely through the mine field laid out for me.

Lord, I leave everything to you, confidently placing my life in your hands, for you've never failed me, O God of integrity and fidelity. You know how I loathe idol-worshipers, how my trust is in you. I'm sure I'll know happiness again once my troubles are ended, once you have shown again how much you love me. You always notice the least of my needs, and my inner turmoil is no secret to you. My enemies have never been able to box me in. No; thanks to you, I always manage to squeak through to open spaces.

But, Lord, come soon, things are desperate. I sit here blinded by tears, huddled in misery, sick to my stomach. All I know is sorrow, all I do is sigh. In punishment for my sins I'm just wasting away, my health is destroyed. My enemies mock me to my face, my neighbors ridicule and taunt me. And my friends—they don't even want to know me, they see me coming and run the other way. I might just as well be dead and gone for all they care; they've tossed me aside like a worn-out shoe. I can sense a whispered campaign being waged against me, I feel it on every side. They're planning to kill me, I know it.

Still—I've faith, Lord, unwavering faith and trust in you, the one I've always acknowledged as Savior. My life is in your hands, save me! Let me bask once more in the sunshine of your favor, show me how good you can be. Don't let me be beaten and disgraced, not after having prayed so hard and so long. Let them be shamed, let them be silenced for good, let them be struck dumb for daring to insult and persecute one of your friends.

Oh, the wonders in store for those who revere and trust in you, those who publicly witness to their faith in you. You shield them by your hidden presence so that no amount of plotting or malicious slander can touch them.

Blessed be God, who has showered so many blessings on me within the shelter of a strongly fortified city. I doubted you once though, Lord; yes, I say it with shame, I really thought you were finished with me. But no, you were there all the time, your saving answer coming through to me, swift and sure.

Love the Lord, you friends of the Almighty. Love him I say. He may make those who get puffed up with pride pay double for their sin but he rewards fidelity handsomely. So take heart, all you whose only hope is in him, and he'll increase your courage. And above all, never give up!

32

WHAT A WONDERFUL FEELING to know your sins are forgiven, that it's all over. What a relief to know that the Lord holds nothing against you anymore, that your conscience is clear again.

For a long time I couldn't unburden myself, I couldn't talk about it. But I could feel my guilt eating me up inside so that, in spite of myself, bitter groans would sometimes betray my inner turmoil. No relief day or night, bowed under the knowledge that it was you, Lord, pressuring me to repent.

I grew weak and sickly, hollowed-eyed and dry-mouthed. Then finally I gave in; unable to bear any more, I broke down and confessed, made a clean breast of the whole thing. I'd said to myself, "I'll go to him . . . confess . . . tell him everything . . . maybe he'll. . . ." And you forgave me! Oh, what joy! We were friends again! What hope and confidence this gives to all transgressors. You do respond, in your own time, if someone is sincere and persevering in prayer. No danger too mortal to be rescued from, no sin too great.

Lord, you're my constant refuge, my bulwark keeping evil at bay. Your voice sings in my soul, encouraging me to hope. "Listen to me," you urge, "I'll show you exactly what to do and the best way to go about it. I'll watch your every move and advise you every step of the way. Don't be a horse or a stubborn mule that has to be securely bridled before you can bend it to your will." Troublemakers are always bringing themselves to a bad end, but those who entrust themselves unconditionally to God come to bask in his favor.

Be happy, you friends of God, shout for joy all you dear good souls!

psalm
33

S HOUT FOR JOY, FAITHFUL ONES, praise is beautiful on the lips of
the chosen. Thank the Lord with song, with your harps and guitars. Compose! Be creative! Pour out wild torrents of melodious gladness! For everything God does is wonderful, and he is unfailingly
faithful to his word. (Isn't this cause for rejoicing?) And how he loves
and rewards fair-dealing and honesty; they impel him to outbursts of
generosity. The evidence of his loving kindness is all around us, can't
you see?

One word from him and the heavens appeared. One rapturous sigh
and they were strewn with stars. The waters were marshaled into vast
oceans; and his reservoirs—bottomless depths. O world, hold him in
greatest awe; peoples of the earth, stand amazed. One simple utterance
and everything simply was, one command and it all materialized,
trembling to do his will.

So who are human beings to contend with him? He has the power
to make hash of all their carefully laid schemes. But his designs
stretch from infinity to infinity, and whatever he's set his heart on
accomplishing has been accomplished. The joy of belonging to such
a God, to be among those he has chosen to be inheritors of his earth!

From above he watches each and every one of us, carefully scruti-
nizing our actions, for after all, humankind is his creation and he can
read the mysteries hidden in every heart—oh, he knows us through
and through. Rulers? Their vast armies can't shield them from his
gaze. Great and mighty warriors? Their strength is useless. Stallions?
The horse hasn't been born that has the strength and speed to carry
it out of his sight.

Yet how kindly God regards his friends, those who hold him in awe, who trust in his mercy and in his ability to rescue them out of every danger.

How deep is our soul's longing for him, for this God who is our support and our defense. What joy it is to trust in him. Dear God, be merciful to us always, we who have put our entire lives in your hands.

I WILL OFFER AN UNCEASING LITANY of praise and glory to the Lord. The exultation of my soul will instill new hope in the despairing. "Yes, come," I will tell them; "Join me in singing praise to the Lord. Sing, friends, take heart! Don't be gloomy!"

How I needed him; I called and called and then the answer came, peace came, deliverance from fear and anxiety. You can hope for this too, just turn to him for help and you'll find yourselves alight with joy. No more need to hide your faces in shame. Why, I know of someone desperate who cried out to God, was heard and saved. Yes, I know this man well.

It is as if God sends angels to form a protective wall around his friends to repel all attack. Try him, see for yourselves how good he is and what happiness there is in store for those who rely solely on him. Revere the Lord, you his special friends; he loves you. What else do you need? The rich can lose everything in a second, be reduced to abject poverty and starvation, but God's friends—never.

Gather round, little ones, let me tell you what the fear of the Lord really is. Is it a long life you want, security? Then watch your tongue. Let every word you say be true, every action open and above board. Avoid bad company, always try to do the right thing. Be peaceable, always try to find peaceful solutions to the problems of life. God is always quick to hear the prayers of the peaceable, but casts a cold eye and turns a deaf ear to the shifty-eyed and devious. *That* for them! From God and everyone else. But when the loyal, the brokenhearted, and the despairing call out to him, he's there in an instant to rescue them. Those who show a real willingness to reform have a real friend in him. The good do have their share of afflictions, of that you can be sure, but with this exception: with the trial comes the way out of it. God watches over them to make sure they come to no great harm.

Hardened sinners? They're broken by their trials; those who persecute the innocent pay very heavily for their crimes. But God grants salvation to his friends; no one who has him to turn to can go far wrong.

psalm
35

O GOD, ANSWER THOSE WHO TAUNT ME, open fire on those who wage war on me. Arm yourself and come to my rescue, mount a blistering counterattack, cut off all escape. Let me hear your comforting voice within me saying, "Trust me, I'll save you."

May shame and disgrace be the lot of my persecutors, let those who are trying to ruin me know nothing but crushing and humiliating defeat. Send avenging angels to sweep them away like dust, driving them along relentlessly down dark and slippery tunnels in payment for this senseless plot against the life of the innocent. As for the ringleaders, may they fall headlong into the trap they set for me. Let them be ambushed and killed. Then, then I can live secure and happy under your protection, a sense of well-being flooding my soul, my whole being, so that all of me exults. O God, there's no one like you. Who else rushes to help the underdog? Who else is friend to the friendless, lover of the unloved?

Look at that crowd of liars lined up to testify against me, ready to accuse me of things I've never even thought of, much less done. To think of it—I was kind to them and this is how they repay me—it breaks my heart. Yes, when they were in desperate straits how I suffered for them—did penance for them—prayed for them on my knees (may my prayers redound to my own good). I wept for them as though for my dearest friend or only sister or brother; I went about chin-on-chest as though my own mother had died.

But let me be the one in trouble and they make coarse jokes about it; they talk me over, even in the presence of strangers, tearing me to pieces. Oh the things they say! Anything to curry favor with my more powerful enemies.

Lord, are you just going to stand there watching? Help me! I tell you, they'd like to tear the very soul out of me. Come to my rescue once more and the whole world will hear of it, I promise. Don't let these undeserved enemies gloat over me, don't let me fall victim to their sly looks and snide remarks. Every word they speak is two-edged. Peace? They've never heard of it. All they live for is intrigue, all they feed on is the blood of the innocent. Lying in their teeth, they taunt me to my face saying, "Come on now, admit it, we saw you do it!" See, Lord? See? Say something! Don't be so distant. Listen to me! Clear me of all these false charges, you who are justice itself. Don't give them a chance to crow over me, saying with malicious glee, "Hey! We did it, we got him this time! He's ruined now for sure!"

Dishonor on those who are glad because of my hard luck, double dishonor and disgrace on all who gloat over me. But abundant blessings on those who did not forget a friend, who never lost faith in me. May they never stop praising God for his goodness to me. And I too will fill my days with divine praises, Lord, and the never-ending account of your love for me.

THE EVIL ARE DRAWN TO SIN like a magnet; they are totally devoid of the fear of God. Sin beguiles them with easy conquests and they flatter themselves into thinking that they will never be found out—until the great unmasking comes. They are, of course, liars and hypocrites, and any good thought that enters their heads dies aborning. Completely given over to depravity, they lie in bed at night thinking up new schemes, new atrocities to perpetrate at the first opportunity. Their consciences are so dulled that the most heinous crimes leave them unmoved.

But thank you, O Lord, for your kindness is as vast as the heavens and as high as the skies. Your righteousness is as steady and immoveable as a mighty mountain, and the mystery of your judgments is as bottomless and unfathomable as the deep blue sea. Why, all creation lies in the palm of your hand. What an inexhaustible treasure-trove of goodness you are, O Lord; just the shadow of your outstretched arms shelters and safeguards all of us. All partake of the riches of your own table, drinking their fill from your abundant stores.

You are the very fountain of life, and it is only by your light that we are enlightened. Please, never stop being good to us, we who know and love you so much. Continue your protection of the honest and upright. Don't let us be trampled underfoot by the proud or manhandled and dispossessed by the ruthless.

There! Look! Look at them—beaten! And this time for good!

D ON'T UPSET YOURSELF over the notorious or bother your head over their escapades. Why envy their apparent successes? These people are only scrub grass—one hot day and they dry up to be blown away by the slightest breeze.

Keep your eyes on God, trust him; be good to others, live quietly where you are, stand your ground no matter what, and keep faith. Enjoy the Lord and he'll answer the innermost yearning of your heart. Put your life in his hands, entrusting all your undertakings to his care, and he'll see you through. Don't worry, everything will come out into the open and your name will be completely cleared. Just leave it all to him; be patient and don't let the outward triumphs of double-dealers and extortionists disturb you. Keep calm or they'll pull you down to their level!

You see those criminals? *That* for them! Oblivion is all they'll get for their pains. But those who go along with God and keep to his ways will reap benefits hand over fist. Just a little while now and those scheming malefactors will disappear; look high and low all you want, you won't find a trace of them. And then, then the gentle, the peacemakers will have the upper hand; the earth will belong to such as these, and they'll breathe deeply of freedom, peace, and contentment.

While oppressors fume and sputter at their would-be victims, God merely laughs, knowing their days are numbered. Unsuspecting, the enemies load themselves down with every conceivable weapon but the tables are suddenly turned on them and . . . they're only a bad memory. How much better it is to have only an honest pittance to live on than ostentatious stores of ill-gotten goods. Thieves face God's wrath but the honest know only the joy of God's protective presence. None of their misfortunes go unnoticed and their holdings are held secure. Nor are they broken by hard times; famine is unknown among them. But sinners—away with them, curses on them! Burn them to a crisp, they and all their evil schemes; let them go up in choking smoke. These people are so ready to "borrow"; oh, so slow to repay. While the kindly, why, they don't merely lend, they give. God blesses his friends, but his enemies . . . down with them! God personally guides his friends' steps in the right paths and watches over their progress with deep delight. If trouble comes, they're not disheartened because they know who their friend is.

Never in my youth, now in my old age, have I known God to desert friends or allow their families to be reduced to penury. Having spent their days spreading kindness, they can be sure their own kin will be provided for. So reform your lives, be kind to everyone, and peace will be with you all your days, yes, and with all who come after you.

How much God loves the just and how loyal he is to his faithful followers. Their names live on and on—while the sinful and treacherous perish without a trace. The law-abiding can be sure of a life of peace on their own land, land that is theirs forever. Words of wisdom come from the just and prudence governs all their decisions, for God's laws are engraved on their hearts and they walk with unwavering stride along the straight and narrow.

But the wicked, green with envy, spy on them and plan their downfall. They don't realize that God isn't about to abandon his friends to their evil scheming or let them be convicted on a lot of trumped-up charges.

Be patient, then, keep with the Lord, and you'll see how he rescues you from your distress and caps it all by settling you on your very own land. And you will have the pleasure of watching the destruction of your enemies before your very eyes.

I saw a man once, a huge boss of a man, arms like tree trunks, dwarfing everything and everyone around him. Then one day—poof— he was gone, disappeared. I looked high and low, not a sign, not a trace remained—understand? So keep your eye on the peaceable; there's a bright future in store for them. But wrongdoers? Mass extinction! Only the gallows await, while God's intimates have him on their side in all their troubles; they just have to cry out to him and he's there. How generously God responds when he knows he is trusted.

O GOD, PLEASE DON'T BE ANGRY with me anymore—please relent. I'm pierced by spasms of burning pain brought on by this crushing punishment, and guilt is eating away at my very bones. This weight of sin is too much for me, it's squeezing the life out of me. I'm a mass of running sores and bent almost double in my agony; my insides feel like they're on fire. Sick, worn out, beaten, I'm unable to check the groans that break from me. You've broken my heart!

O Lord, do I have to tell you the state I'm in? One look should suffice. Shaking drains away what little strength I've got left; I can't see straight anymore. And to add to all of this, my supposed friends won't come near me now—afraid of contamination I suppose. My dear relatives watch warily—from a safe distance. Then there are my enemies . . . just waiting for their chance to finish me off. They've set up elaborate traps for me and concocted all kinds of evil with which to plague me; false charges, perjury mean nothing to them.

But their threats fall on deaf ears and I don't attempt to refute their calumnies—they might as well curse a stone. I'll respond only to your voice, Lord, for it is you and you alone I'm longing for and from whom I await salvation. "Please, Lord," I plead, "come soon or they'll gloat over me, laughing up their sleeves over my apparent misfortune!"

I'm in such misery, I'm so close to the end of my rope, in constant pain. I know, I know, I'm guilty, I admit it—that's why remorse is tearing me apart. Still, look at them, dyed-in-the-wool criminals but in the pink of health. Incredible. And my swarm of enemies grows hourly. My former friends, those who received so many favors from me—this is how they repay me, by becoming my enemies, by hating me for trying to live right.

O God, don't you turn on me; come back to me, Lord, save me— and soon, Lord, make it soon!

I PROMISED MYSELF I WOULDN'T SAY ANYTHING. I said to myself, "Don't lose your temper, you'll only talk yourself into more trouble. Don't say a word while they're present." So I just stood there and took it; even though it gave precious little comfort, I made no effort to defend myself—swallowing every bitter retort—but inside I was boiling mad, my anger like a ball of fire within me that kept growing larger and larger until, as I brooded over the injustice of it all, suddenly, in a blinding burst of hurt rage, unleashing my tongue, I exploded. . . .

"God," I roared, "how much longer? Is this what you call living? Tell me, when is it all going to end? Tell me it won't be long now. What good are these few miserable days on earth? Compared with yours, my lifespan doesn't amount to a thing. Even at its best, humanity is a nothing, a nothing, emptiness and hollow show. We rush around, poor fools, like headless chickens, darting here and there in a senseless lather, piling up possessions we don't know what to do with once we have them. I ask you, is this living?"

"Lord, you're all I have. Save me from myself, from my sinfulness and weakness. Don't let me become the butt of obscene jokes. I didn't answer them back, did I? I said nothing; I recognize that it's you who in some mysterious way and for some mysterious reason are letting this happen to me. Mercy, Lord, make it stop, Lord; you've hammered me practically into the ground! When you decide to make people pay for their sins, you can really wither them with your reproof and strip them of their blown-up ideas about themselves. Oh yes, vanity gets us all in the end.

"Lord, I'm on my knees, begging you, crying like a baby. We seem to have become strangers to each other; I'm reduced to a nomad's existence, like my ancestors before me. Aiee! Turn those accusing eyes from me for the space of a breath or I'm finished!"

psalm 40

A T LAST, AT LAST, AN ANSWER TO MY PRAYERS, my patience has been rewarded! God reached down into the quicksand of troubles swallowing me and swooped me up in his arms, setting me squarely and securely on my feet again. What joy, what outpouring of happy songs, what praises poured from me. All who heard about it with wonder were encouraged to take heart and renew their trust in him.

What blessings are in store for those who trust only in God, who haven't thrown in their lot with idolaters to advance their ends. O God, the things you've done for us. You're beyond compare, no word of mine could ever begin to do you justice. Showy sacrifices don't impress you—you've shown me that—and abundance isn't important when it comes to offerings of reparation. What you want is an open ear, attentive, listening. Very well, Lord, since it isn't sacrifices or victims that you're seeking—take me. I offer you myself. You want obedience? Here's mine. Nothing could make me happier than to do whatever you want with all my heart.

Everyone knows how I feel, I've shouted it from the housetops; you know that. Every single thing you've ever done for me is public knowledge. I count on this being in my favor now that I need help so badly. I want to draw from your inexhaustible fount of compassion, to be unerringly guided by your love and your truth because, shame to say, I've failed again. Through my own fault troubles as numerous as the hairs on my head have rained down on me and I see no way out of them. I've completely lost heart.

Help me, Lord, please; once again, frustrate those who are thirsting for my blood. Turn the tables on them for a change. Let their loud mocking laughter become howls of rage and defeat. While those who have never lost faith in you and ever experienced your help fill the air with your praises. Yes, I may be a nobody, but not to my God. You are my friend, O Lord, so please come, come soon; I need you so!

THOSE WHO LOOK AFTER the down and out are the lucky ones; when they themselves need help, God will be quick to come to their rescue. And he'll keep them under his protection, to their great good fortune, not letting them fall into the hands of any enemy. If they fall ill they'll be healed—they might lie down as sick as a dog but soon they'll be up and about, hale and hearty.

I've experienced this myself, so I know. A terrible illness had attacked me; I prayed, "I'm sick, Lord; hear the prayer of a poor sinner. They've all given up on me. Listen to them out there, the hypocrites. 'How long do you think he has, when are we going to be rid of him?' Oh yes, they come to visit me, wringing their hands, but in their heads they're counting the days. Once outside they talk me over; I can hear them. 'It's a cancer, of course, hasn't a chance in the world. A man's sins do catch up with him don't they? He won't be leaving that bed alive!' And what hurts most of all is that my own best friend is out there among them, adding his mockery to theirs! After all the good times we had together. Why, my house was his house.

O God, be good to me, get me out of this bed so I can pay them all back. You can prove your love for me by helping me to undermine all their plans to get rid of me. My past fidelity must count for something!"

Blessed be the God of Israel, throughout all the ages, amen—amen—amen—amen!

Book II

Psalms 42–72

M Y SOUL THIRSTS FOR YOU, O God, just like a doe thirsts for a bubbling spring. My soul is parched with desire for God, so vibrantly alive. How long before I can feast my eyes on Almighty God? Tears are all the nourishment I have from day to day; I run the gauntlet of their jeers, "Come on, where is this God of yours, huh?"

In my grief my mind harkens back to better times; oh how good it was then. Those joyful celebrations, those happy pilgrimages, those processions into the temple with me at the head, singing and leaping, the crowd delirious with joy! My poor soul, why so depressed, why these shuddering sighs? Let us trust God! It will all be given back to us one day. I'll sing again, glorify him again.

But now, how sad I am. My thoughts keep turning to the past, from this place of exile here east of the Jordan, to Mount Hermon and the hills of Mizar. The melting snows of Mount Hermon that swell the Jordan are like the troubles that toss and fling me about mercilessly. God, it almost seems as if you have inundated me with miseries. But no, your mercies are renewed day by day so that even in the loneliness of the night there is the faint echo of a song in my heart, moving me to prayer and entreaty. I ask, "Why, Lord, why have you allowed this? Why this seeming indifference to my misery? It breaks me in half to have to listen to the taunts they fling in my face, 'And where's your dear friend now?'"

My poor soul, why so depressed, why these heavy sighs? Trust him I tell you. I know I will sing songs of praise again, glorifying my God and Savior.

psalm

43

PLEASE, LORD, DEFEND ME. The whole world's against me; lies are being spread about me. I need your help; you're all I have. How can you remain so unconcerned? Don't cut me off. Why should I have to drag myself around all day, victimized, intimidated, mercilessly persecuted? Throw some light on this, show me what to do, where to turn; that's all I ask. Bring me home again, back to the heights where you dwell.

Then I can once more come as a pilgrim to the altar of my God, he who is the source and wellspring of my joy. What songs of thanksgiving, what tunes I'll play on my guitar.

Why so sad, O my soul, what does all this groaning mean? Don't lose hope. All will be well again soon. I'll fill the air with songs of praise—exalting him who is the song in my heart.

44

O GOD, WHAT A WONDERFUL STORY our ancestors tell us. What tales of the marvels you did for us in the old days. Why, with your bare hands you demolished unbelieving nations in order to establish us, dealing out deadly punishment on the godless. The land was blanketed with our people, as far as the eye could see.

Was it our strength, our prowess that won all this for us? Far from it—it was you, Lord, only your love for us that accomplished it. O my God, you say just the word and Jacob is saved. It's only because of you that we are enabled to overrun the enemy, only because of you that we can trample them underfoot. Could I be so foolish as to trust in my own meager resources or skills? Salvation comes from you alone; only you are able to humble our persecutors into the ground as they deserve. You, O God, have been our daily miracle and we can never stop thanking you, never.

But—Lord—what is this—you seem to have abandoned us, throwing us into a state of confusion. Our armies, bereft of your support, now suffer loss after shameful loss.

We flee the scene of battle like scared rabbits. Overrun by the enemy, our camps are looted and destroyed; no one offers even token resistance. They herd us together like animals to be led away to slaughter, or else we are ruthlessly dispossessed and scattered far and wide. How little you value your people, practically giving us away, cheap as dirt. You let everyone and anyone heap abuse on us, and even our former friends and neighbors enjoy themselves at our expense. We're the butt of universal ridicule; there isn't anyone who hasn't had a good laugh over us.

It's all I can think about. My face burns with such shame that I can't even raise my head, much less attempt to refute the lying insults flung at us so contemptuously. And why? What have we done to deserve all this, except cling to our faith in you and follow your law to the letter? It took courage but we never wavered, even when we didn't understand and you seemed to be leading us straight into oblivion. If we had taken to idol-worship and denied you, could you possibly not know it? Why, our very hearts are an open book to you. No, it's because of our fidelity that we suffer now, and nothing else, it's because of this that we're marked for attack.

Can you be asleep, Lord? Then rouse yourself, don't disown us completely! How can you turn your back on us, ignoring our dire need? We're humbled into the dust, crawling on our bellies. Come to our rescue and save us, for pity's sake, as a sign of your love!

MY HEART IS SO FILLED to overflowing with beautiful words that only a love letter will do. O my King! May my tongue do him justice, may it race along as nimbly as a pen in the hand of the most skillful of transcribers. Here goes!

> O my love, you are head and shoulders above everyone else,
>   your eloquence is unsurpassed.
> No wonder God's blessings rain down upon you, and on all
>   your kin.
> Arm yourself great warrior, strap your shining sword about
>   your slender hips,
> And resplendent in glory and majesty, ride out in triumph,
>   you champion of truth, goodness, and justice.
> When you take aim with your mighty bow, your hand, that in-
>   vincible right hand, inspires dread!
> Your arrows, bright and sharp, clear a swath before you, and
>   your enemies collapse, more in dismay than anything else.
> No one can deprive you of your God-given throne; your reign
>   stands, inflexible as a steel scepter, for true justice.
> You champion justice, detest evil—that is why God fills your
>   heart with such unbounded joy.
> That is why you are the most blessed among all the rulers of
>   the earth; your very robes emit the heady scent of choice
>   spices.
> As you approach to claim your bride, melodious stringed music
>   wafts through the air from ivory palaces in soul-tingling
>   songs of welcome.
> And the bride herself; surely the most beautiful among the
>   maidens who accompany her, all of them royal princesses.
> There she stands, at your right, splendid in gold of Ophir.

As for you, my dear, listen carefully—forget the past now, forget the old country, your parents and kin. A sovereign is in love with you. You belong to him now and it is to him that you owe complete allegiance. Honor him as lord and master.

And look there, O daughter of Tyre, see where they come; the entire city has turned out in your honor. Among them are the wealthiest, loaded down with every conceivable gift, vying with one another for a scrap of attention, some small favor from your hand.

How radiantly beautiful is this royal princess, reclining in her ornate chamber, dressed in her sumptuous golden robe. Her cloak, encrusted with pearls, spreads richly as she is borne out with ceremony along a richly carpeted aisle to be presented to her groom; on either side a double row of maidens forms her honor guard and the crowd goes wild with joy at their appearance. To the sound of drums and the blaring of trumpets the colorful procession solemnly enters the palace of the king.

O king, your dynasty is never-ending; your sons and their sons after them will wear royal crowns. I will see to it that your praises are sung through the ages so that all nations will honor you, forever and ever.

psalm 46

GOD IS ALWAYS ON OUR SIDE, always there when we need him—so what is there to fear? Even if our whole world crumbles about us, sending the mountains crashing into the depths of the sea, creating gigantic tidal waves and undermining the very foundations of the earth.

God is there I tell you, he's always there.

Peace is like a river, its flowing waters bringing joy in abundance to Zion, God's city, surely the holiest of places. With God in its midst, nothing can shake it; the light of dawn always finds him at his post, hovering protectingly, lovingly, over his darling. There is turmoil and unrest everywhere, nations at each other's throats—one word from him and the world crumbles.

God is here, I tell you, God is always here.

Look. Look at all the wonderful things God has done, incredible marvels, too many to count. Conflicts cease, weapons are splintered, war machines go up in flames. "Stop!" he thunders; "Admit that I'm your God. Give me my due honor, all you nations; celebrate my praises, all you children of the earth."

Our God is there, I tell you, he's always there.

EVERYBODY! CLAP YOUR HANDS, come on, shout it out, praise the
Lord! Stomp! Leap! God, Almighty God—how tremendous he
is, the whole earth is his realm. And he's made everyone on it subject
to us, made all the nations ours to walk on. We've come into our
hand-picked inheritance, Canaan, the pride and joy of Jacob.

Listen to the tumultuous ovation as God takes his seat upon his
royal throne, the trumpets blowing for all they're worth, blast after
mighty blast!

> Sing God's praises, sing him songs of praise.
> Sing our Lord's praises, play him songs of praise.

The whole earth is his domain, so celebrate with songs of worship.
God rules gloriously over the earth from his holy throne, and royal
emissaries of all the nations have come together to pay him homage,
to join voices with the people of God in swearing allegiance to him.

He is master of all, to him be glory!

48

GOD IS WONDERFUL, UTTERLY WORTHY of the praises showered upon him by his very own city, Jerusalem. This Jerusalem, beautifully set on Mount Zion like a glistening jewel—it is our pride, our joy, a city worthy of our great Lord.

God's protective presence resides within its walls, keeping her from harm. When besiegers encircled her menacingly, what they saw left them stunned and shaken. Panic-stricken they raced away; falling into fits of trembling, they clutched at themselves, convulsed like a woman in labor. Their ordered ranks broke up in confusion, as when a sudden, violent east wind sweeps the waves of the sea. God snapped their powerful army in two as easily as a ship is splintered in a howling storm.

So everything we heard is really true! Everything in God's holy city is just as they told us. It is an eternal empire, God's empire. O Lord, we've long pondered these truths, meditated long in your holy temple. It's only right to give praise to so great a God, a God so ready to defend the poor and humble against the arrogant. Mount Zion, celebrate! Juda, rejoice! Because everything God does is right.

Walk the length and breadth of Zion, examine every part of it. Count all its towers and massive fortifications. Inspect its palatial homes, superb showplaces, so that you can give an eyewitness account of all these marvels to future generations. So that they will know, as we know, that this God is our God and he will be our infallible guide forever.

49

GATHER ROUND, ALL YOU PEOPLE, bend an ear, nations of the world—celebrity or nobody, rich or poor, no distinctions. I've some sound words of advice to offer, the fruit of long hours of meditation. As I pluck musingly on the strings of my guitar, I'll unravel a riddle revealed to me.

These were my thoughts: Should I be shaken when hard times come and enemies abound? Be afraid of the rich and powerful who think money can buy anything and boast of it? Not likely! No amount of money on earth can buy life—God can't be bribed. Gold can't save you from death; it's utterly futile to entertain such thoughts. Live forever? Never taste death? Ridiculous.

Everybody dies, we know that. Brilliant or dense, wise or foolish, all go down the same road—to oblivion—and all their greedy gain is left in the grasp of others; their graves are their palaces, forever. But they try to console themselves by saying they'll at least live on through their vast holdings and descendants, by passing on their titles and estates. Such conceit. Everything they prided themselves on avails them nothing—it might as well be a dog that died.

This is how those fools think, and those who are swayed by their opinions are twice as dumb. They'll all be hustled into the grave like a herd of frightened sheep, with stark Death as their gruesome shepherd. Then the downtrodden will at last have the upper hand while these villains rot in the grave—no more need for palatial homes. God preserve me from such a fate. I've every hope that in the end I'll be saved.

So listen to me, friends, don't let the apparent successes of the vicious dismay you. When you see them piling up riches and adding fortune to fortune, you can be sure they'll have to drop everything when Death comes. Even though they might have enjoyed patting themselves on the back and crowing, "Congratulations, you're top dog now, everyone looks up to you!" they're doomed to the darkness of death just as all who went before and will come after.

Mortals, for all their earthly grandeur, if they've got no sense will miss the whole point of living, for humans have no more hold on life than a dumb beast.

psalm
50

G OD, THE ALMIGHTY, the Holy One, speaks. From horizon to
horizon he summons the earth to account. His light blazes
forth from the heights of beautiful Mount Zion. Yes, our God is coming, and not by stealth. No, flames shoot out from him, heralding his
approach; howling winds and pelting rains form his honor guard.
Heaven and earth are summoned to witness the accounting he is to
exact from his people.

"Stand forth!" he thunders. "Bring me my saints! Those who entered into a sacred covenant with me through the sacrifice of sheep
and oxen." The heavens rumble approval and praise their Creator,
testifying to his supreme right of judgment.

"Listen, my people, to what I'm about to say," he continues. "And
you, Israel, prepare to hear my verdict on you. I speak as God, your
God. It's not your sacrificial offerings that displease me; oh no, not
one burnt offering have I rejected. But then, what need do I have for
your bulls or fat goats? All creation is mine. I can lay claim to cattle
by the thousands, entire mountains can be clothed in steers. Mine,
everything that flies, walks, or crawls. Do you imagine I'd need to
come to you for food if I were hungry, when I have the entire universe at my disposal? Am I nourished by the meat of bulls or do I
slake my thirst with goat's blood? Praise is the offering that satisfies
me; promises fulfilled, vows kept, these are what I want. Then when
you need me, I'll be more disposed to help you, and this in its turn
will bring fresh outbursts of praise from your lips.

"But you," God says, turning to the false-hearted, "you hypocrites,
what do you mean standing there preaching justice and love, mouth-
ing my laws, while all the time nothing can curb you as you trample
decency underfoot? You frequent the hangouts of thieves and rub
elbows with idolaters. You indulge in foul talk and lying has become

second nature to you. You sit there, two-faced, tearing your sisters and brothers apart, destroying the name and reputation of your own. Do you think I'm blind as well as deaf? Or perhaps you dare to think of me as a kindred spirit, you presumptuous wretches. Watch out, because I'm going to face you with all of this!"

"Mark my words, all of you who go your merry way without a thought for me, or you'll fall into my hands and no one will lift a finger to help you. But those who offer sacrifices of praise are a credit to me; I'll reveal myself to those who keep to the straight and narrow."

O GOD, HAVE MERCY, in your goodness and kindness, forgive me. Wash me clean of these terrible stains of sin and guilt. Yes, I admit it, I've done wrong, and I'm tortured by the memory of it. And it's against you that I've done this, it's you who have been the target of my perfidy because I knew very well what's absolutely loathsome to you—and did it anyway. You were right, completely justified in condemning me.

I was born bad, bad from the first moment of my existence. Goodness is what pleases you, I know that; but you'll have to teach me, Lord, remake me from the inside out. Oh, with you on my side, and under your purifying action, how clean and white my soul will be again, like the purest whitest snow!

Put new life into me, Lord, give me the joy and gladsomeness that comes from a clear conscience. Then I'll be able to shake off this weight of sorrow that threatens to crush me altogether. Cloak my sins with your mercy; no, blot them out completely as if they never were. I need a new heart and a fresh surge of courage. Please don't send me away, depriving me of all sense of your strengthening presence. I want to be happy, full of docility and innocence.

Think of how much I can do for others who are in need, how I can help them in the same predicament. Oh, to have to live knowing I'm a murderer. Dear God, release me from this oppressive weight of guilt. Help me sing the wonders of your mercy. Open my lips, give me words so I can praise you as you deserve. I know that animal sacrifices add nothing to your glory, that burnt offerings don't move you. If they could I'd certainly be quick to offer them up. No, what you demand is contrition, the breaking of an arrogant and proud spirit; you'll never turn your back on the truly repentant.

God, restore poor war-ravaged Zion, rebuild her crumbling walls. Then, we'll once again be able to offer you pleasing sacrifices, offered in the right spirit—untainted offerings, whole and entire, the choicest bullocks for your altar.

psalm 52

WHY PARADE YOUR EVIL PAST, master-criminal? God's mercy outshines your accomplishments. You enjoy cutting others to pieces with your vicious tongue, don't you? Why, you're as sharp and destructive as a straight razor! You positively revel in your evilness, lying is pure joy for the likes of you. What you like best is tearing people down, trampling their names and reputations underfoot, while decent and honest dealing bores you to tears.

Well, prepare yourself, you dregs of viciousness, God's going to deal with you himself and that'll mean the end. Oh yes, the rug'll suddenly be pulled from under you, all you relied on, all your props, gone in a wink—right down to your very life itself. This will be staggering to behold; even those loyal to God will be taken aback by the suddenness of it all. But then—amid gales of triumphant laughter—they'll roar, "Well, look at that! So this is the one who was Mr. Independent? Who trusted only in money and its power to buy instead of the Almighty and who just went from bad to worse? Well, well."

But as for me, I've found fulfillment in the Lord; I'm like a healthy tree, leafy and sturdy. I trust him with my life, to the end of my days. Yes, Lord, in deep unending gratitude I'll wait patiently, silently for even more blessings, and my very being will be a living witness to your goodness for all who see me.

psalm

53

ONLY A FOOL WOULD DENY the existence of God. Only hopeless fools lead lives of crime, committing acts of violence—oh, there's not a shred of decency among them. God scrutinizes human-kind from above in the hope of discovering at least one who cares about the salvation of his soul; but no, they've all taken the same road to perdition. Not one—hard to believe it, but not one—with a wholesome thought.

When are they going to come to their senses, these people who fatten themselves on the weak and helpless and never give a thought to God? Are these criminals senseless, chewing up their victims like so many loaves of bread? Yet there's no real reason to dread them. God will cause the bones of your tormentors to whiten in the sun, O Israel; you will triumph over them because God is on your side. Oh, to know who it is who will come from Zion to save us!

When it happens, Jacob will jump for joy and all Israel will ring with jubilant laughter.

O GOD HELP ME! By your name and strength, be my judge. Bend your ear to my prayer, to my desperate pleading. Strange enemies are arising against me on every side; and there's a bloodthirsty panting for my life, those who are ruthless, totally without conscience sniff me out.

But wait, God is near, supporting and strengthening me; he'll turn the tables on them. Demolish them, O Lord, O Judge and Executioner! And in gratitude I'll joyfully offer up choice sacrifices; loud will be my praises of your holy name.

Oh, how good it is! Once again God has used his great power to come between me and certain disaster, destroying my enemies before my very eyes.

55

OH GOD, HEAR MY PLEA—no, don't turn a deaf ear, listen, please, and answer me; I'm at the end of my rope. I shake in my boots at the mere thought of the danger threatening me. They pursue me relentlessly, their hatred fueled by their raging anger. Death stares me in the face, my blood runs cold and my hands are clammy from sheer terror.

If only I had some place to run to, if I could just sprout wings and fly off, out to the middle of a vast desert. I'd be safe there, I could breathe again, safe from the storm of abuse that's broken over my head.

Cover them with confusion, Lord, set them at one another's throats! The city's become a jungle; violence is the order of the day and citizens cower behind closed and bolted doors. Everywhere there's graft, fear, and corruption. But if this was all I had to contend with, I could somehow stand it. If I had been bested in fierce competition by a bitter and ruthless rival, even that I could bear. But this. How could you do this, you, my best friend. After all our good times together— we laughed, talked, even prayed together. Why, you were my other self.

Damn them all, to hell with them! Let them be buried alive! They revel in evil, give them their fill! But I—I swear it—I'll never turn away from my God, I'll never stop needing him and pleading for his guidance. I'll pray unceasingly, morning, noon, and night, and I know he'll hear me. In the midst of all my troubles I know deep peace. Even though I might be outnumbered ten to one, I remain serene. Why? Because it's God who's fighting for me, God. You hear? God who's going to rescue me and grind them into the dirt. He'll do this by his mighty power, smashing those who are utterly without conscience.

And my so-called friend? That one has betrayed all of us. Lied under oath, trampled every promise underfoot. Oh, that one can flatter, but with a heart full of treachery. Words as smooth as silk, but they'll cut you to pieces. Be warned! Trust in God alone and he'll never fail you.

O God, condemn all evil-doers to the fate they deserve. Cut them off in the full bloom of life, at the height of their corruption. But let me trust in you forever!

56

MERCY, O LORD, MERCY; be good to me, Lord, they're after me. Not a moment of peace as they press their attack round the clock. Pitfalls wherever I turn, an army of enemies pursuing me. But—just when I'm about to collapse in despair, I remember you and take heart. It moves me to acts of trust, adoration, and praise. It gives me strength, calms my fears. What can they do to me? What can puny finite beings do against my God?

But see how clever they are, how they sabotage all my plans. My total ruination is an obsession with them, the main topic of all their clandestine meetings. Snakelike, they spy on me, watch my every move, just waiting for their chance to get me.

But will they succeed? Never. O Lord, give them what they deserve. I know you will because you've been with me through thick and thin, haven't you. Not one tear of mine has escaped your notice, not one sorrow, every misfortune carefully recorded in your own hand. That's why my persecutors are finished before they even start. Why, they turn tail and scatter in panic when they hear me cry out to you for help.

I know beyond any doubt that God is championing my cause. He, justice itself—Oh praise him! Mercy itself—Oh glorify him! Knowing this, I'm wholly without fear. Who would dare attack me now?

Dear God, I've committed myself to you, I'll keep my promise to the letter. With thanksgiving offerings I'll make acknowledgment of your saving deeds. Haven't you snatched me from the jaws of death, even kept the very ground under my feet smooth so I can pursue a devout life, free of obstacles and burdens?

PITY ME, LORD, PITY ME, I have no one but you. Let me hide in your protective shadow until all danger is past.

My cries rise up to the Master of the universe; he can do anything. He reaches down from heaven itself to pluck me out of distress, to exonerate me when they smear my name with lies and false charges. What trouble I'm in! I feel like I'm surrounded by roaring lions; I can hear them in my sleep. Like beasts my enemies sink their lying teeth into me, cutting me to pieces with slander. Show them your power O God, show them your glory in all its splendor.

Oh, the traps they have concocted. How can they be so cruel? It sickens me to think about it. But all their craftiness will come to nothing and they'll be the ones caught like rats in their own traps.

I'm ready, Lord, ready to do whatever you ask. Songs of praise? I'll sing my heart out for you. Up, my soul; up, you joyful instruments of song; we're going to raise up a sunrise! I want everyone to hear my song of praise. I want the whole world to resound with my song of thanksgiving. Your mercy is as vast as the heavens, your trustworthiness as high as the sky.

O God, outshine the heavens! O God, bathe the earth in glory!

58

S O YOU THINK YOU KNOW IT ALL, do you? Who gives you the right to sit in judgment on others? False judgments are what you produce out of your black hearts as you scheme hour after hour to bend justice to your will and victimize the innocent. Born bad! Born liars! Your words drip poison, like the venom of snakes. Your minds are completely closed to the whispering of conscience. Snakes who resist the enticements of snake-charmers by stuffing their tails in their ears.

O God, smash in their teeth, maim these young lions beyond all hope! Let them disappear like water running down a drain. When they force their attack, let all their weapons turn back on them. May they ooze away like a slimy snail and be ejected like a miscarriage! May all their carefully laid and devilish plans never know fruition but be swept ruthlessly aside.

Then the just will say, "How sweet it is! Vengeance at last!" Then there'll be enough of the enemy's blood to wade in! Then they can truly say, "Yes, there is a God! Yes, there is justice!"

psalm
59

S AVE ME FROM MY ENEMIES, O God, give me a safe perch way up
high where they can't reach me. Come between me and those
thirsting for my blood. Look at the elaborate network of pitfalls
they've concocted. They openly and brazenly discuss me and how to
do me in—and what have I done to them? Nothing. My conscience is
clear. They've devised this persecution against me without the slightest provocation on my part. Please Lord, wake up, look at what they're
doing. Since you're Lord of lords and God of Israel, surely you've got
the power to deal out punishment; so be merciless to the merciless!

Howling like mad dogs, they return to the attack each night, ter-
rorizing the city from end to end. Blasphemous oaths pour from their
mouths; they have no fear of retribution—"Who's to hear us?" they
snarl. But you just laugh at them, don't you, Lord? Their threats are
nothing but a farce to you. Confident of your power, I await certain
rescue—with you I'm safe.

My merciful God will appear, and swooping me up in his arms,
he'll show me what becomes of my adversaries. Death? No, that's too
easy; once they're dead and gone, people might just forget their
crimes. No, Lord, drive these killers from their lairs, make an example of them, beat them into the ground, O protecting God. Let
them be condemned by the words of their own lips, let their brazen
self-confidence be their undoing, let their lies and false oaths be
gathered together like a net in which to trap them. Cripple their ca-
pacity to hurt and destroy so they know for certain that there's a God
in Jacob, and over all the earth.

Let them return to the attack night after night if they will, howling like the mad dogs they are, prowling the streets and combing the
city for their victim until the crack of dawn—fruitlessly. The rising

sun will find me safe and sound, singing for sheer joy at my escape, rejoicing in my salvation, O Lord, jubilant because once again you've come between me and bitter death.

O God, my strength, I'll worship you with songs of praise. God, my Refuge, my Merciful Savior!

psalm
60

G OD—YOU'VE DISOWNED US, you've pulled the props out from
under us in your anger. Please take us back. You've rocked the
country to its very foundations, gaping fissures and crumbling walls
everywhere. Heal, O God; the entire nation is near complete collapse!

You've really put us up against it this time, forcing us to drink the
bitter cup of oppression to the dregs. We're drunk with sorrow. But
wait, we still have one hope, our covenant, that blessed promise of
old, which we cling to with all our might, our one boast. A standard
we hold aloft proudly for all to see. And so, Lord, since we dare to
believe that we're your darlings, save us by your overwhelming might
in answer to our prayers, our desperate cries for help.

The majesty of his reply, the absolute certainty of his word—"It
will be my special joy to parcel out to you Shechem and the valley of
Succoth. They are mine, mine, just as Gilead and Manasseh are mine.
Ephraim is like a trusty steel helmet, while Judah stands as a sign of
my royal prerogatives—a mighty scepter. But Moab? Moab's just an
old washtub for my feet. And Edom? I'll simply walk in and take it.
The Philistines will be the crowning victory, adding zest to the feast."

This is all very well and good, but . . . when? Where's my
Leader, who's going to open the way for me into Edom? You seem to
have abandoned us, Lord; our armies flounder helplessly in the field,
bereft of your protection. You must come to our rescue or it's all over,
we're finished. From ordinary human beings we can expect less than
nothing.

Only God can save us. Only God can give us the strength to mop
the floor with our enemies.

psalm

61

O GOD, LISTEN TO ME, LISTEN, PLEASE—be open to the lament I raise to you from my bitter exile. I'm so far, so very far from home—it's breaking my heart. Hold out a helping hand to guide me to a safe perch, well out of danger. You are my only hope, the only thing between me and the relentless battle being waged against me. A mighty tower, an unscalable tower. Oh, if only I could rest there forever, safe under your protection. After all, you've accepted my vows, you've given me a share in everything you promised to those who give you due honor.

Grant the king a long and prosperous reign, spanning many generations. May the royal line extend unbroken down through the ages. May mercy and truth stand like guardian angels over him, preserving him from harm like the palace guard.

Then my songs of praise will extend to all eternity because I can honor my vows anew each day.

psalm
62

MY SOUL FINDS REST ONLY IN GOD, only with him do I feel completely safe. No one else can help me, he's everything.

Yet they continue to batter a person mercilessly until all he resembles is a sagging old fence. Worse still, a bulldozed wall. How they long to dethrone me, to strangle me in a network of vicious lies. Fawning and servile to my face, oh yes, but behind the grinning teeth, stinking curses.

My poor soul, let's trust in God alone, let's put all our hope in him. I draw all my strength from him, he's the source of my unshakable confidence. He's my one boast, my joy; I can rely on his support, unmovable as a rock. Listen to me, you Israelites, everyone of you, throw in your lot with him, confide completely in him, pour out your hearts in all simplicity. He will help you.

The high and mighty of this world, who are they after all? Less than nothing. Their accumulated strength? Nothing but a puff of wind, absolutely weightless. Don't be impressed by them, their so-called power, their hoards of extorted wealth, their cheap victories. God has said over and over that he's the source and wellspring of power.

How true it is, Lord—you are all merciful as well, and you deal out to each one of us exactly what we've got coming.

psalm
63

YOU'RE MINE, GOD, I'm on fire with longing for you. I ache all over with it and my soul is one endless stretch of dry hot sand, parched, half-dead. My eyes strain hungrily toward your sanctuary, hoping for even the briefest glimpse of you, for just one look at your radiant glory.

Oh, I love you more than life itself; all I live for is to keep repeating, "I love you . . ." again and again. I want to spend the rest of my days saying it, shouting it out, arms flung wide—pleading hands outstretched. You're the food of my soul, I fairly live on you! Divine praises tumble from my lips in happy bubbling torrents.

At night I lie sleepless for sheer joy, thinking of you as the hours pass unnoticed. All your past kindnesses come to mind, the endless forgiveness, the many times you've rescued me from certain death; cries of love and gratitude break from me over and over. My soul passionately cleaves to you, and your hand presses me closer still.

My bloodthirsty enemies are sure to be thwarted, they're going to wind up exactly where they're trying to send me. The tables will be turned on them and their own swords will cut them down until they're nothing but rotting meat for vultures. But our ruler—what joys are in store for him under God's protection, reveling in the blessings bestowed on all who swear allegiance to him, while liars will have their mouths shut for good.

psalm 64

DEAR GOD, LISTEN TO MY CRIES FOR HELP, to my tale of woe. Stand between me and this terrifying specter. Shelter me from the lies and calumnies that fall about me like a hailstorm, from plots of evil connivers who are coming at me like a howling mob.

They tongue-lash me mercilessly, they sink their insults into my soul like so many poisoned arrows. Underhanded attack is their specialty, sudden ambush of the innocent and unsuspecting. At their secret meetings they snort gleefully over their conquests, egging each other on to more and more acts of brutality. "Who's going to know?" they hiss. "We've got a perfect scheme, we've got it all figured out to the last detail; they haven't been able to hide from us!"

But God knows. The tables will be turned on them and they'll find themselves suddenly riddled with burning arrows—wiped out, every one of them. Onlookers will stand there terrified, stunned and shaken. Then people will finally understand what has happened and who has done it. Then there will be shouts of jubilation, with everyone flocking to God's standard.

And then the downtrodden will raise their heads once more and glory in their God.

65

B LESSED LORD, WE WAIT BEFORE YOU in a silence throbbing with joyful expectation, ready and eager to fulfill our promises. Your answers to our petitions have encouraged all humankind to turn to you.

My sins are many, I know it, the guilt quite crushes me; O forgive us all, Lord, we need your mercy. What a blessing it is to win a place close to you, in your own house. What joys, what riches of grace. May we be allowed our share of these treasures, O Lord, within your holy temple.

How munificently you respond to our needs, O God our Savior, what wonder-working on our behalf. The word of it flashes around the world, across mighty oceans, filling every ear.

The mountains are yours, each set in place by your hand, each magnificent in its snowcapped beauty and power. The seas are yours, with their mountainous crashing waves that can be stilled in a moment at the mere sound of your voice, just as a sudden hush falls upon a multitude. The peoples of the four corners of the earth are struck dumb with awe at the sight of these wonders. From sunrise to sunset the air reverberates with one great shout of joy.

How solicitous you are over Mother Earth, how tenderly you watch over it so that it does not lack for life-giving water to insure abundant crops. From your heavenly reservoir you send the blessings of rain. Why, you seem to have labored over the land yourself, directing these sweet waters along the furrows, shoring and firming up the ridges lest a drop be wasted, breaking up the stubborn clods that they may drink in seed and water, nurturing the tender green shoots as they appear.

And from all this loving care—a bumper crop! A heavy yield spilling out onto the roads at harvest time. Even untilled fields produce crops, making the whole countryside a riot of joyous vegetation. Livestock clothes the meadows, and the valleys are one vast blanket of colorful produce.

Everywhere, singing and shouts of exultation!

psalm

66

COME ON, WORLD, shout for joy! Join voices in songs of praise! Sing your glorious best to his name. Talk to him! Say, "How great you are, everything you do is wonderful! Even your enemies have to admit it as they come cringing into your presence. The whole earth is at your feet. One mighty song rises to heaven in praise of your holy name."

Look, everyone, look at what he has done in our very midst, how awesome his power. One word from him and the sea was no more—dry land from shore to shore—and over they went in perfect safety. What cause for celebration here! His reign is endless, his power un-challenged. Yet he watches over us, our every movement, with un-blinking gaze, lest anyone rebel.

Let's bless God, friends, let's really make ourselves heard! Look, we're safe, free, alive, all because of him. He may have put us to the test, tried us in a crucible of suffering, just as silver is plunged into the fire to remove the impurities. Oh yes, we've been imprisoned, trussed up, mercilessly oppressed, burnt out, flooded, but—at last, at last, it's over. Over!

So here I am, Lord, with my thanksgiving offerings, ready to honor the vows I made in the midst of my anguish. Here's the best of my livestock, the fattest of my sheep, oxen, and goats, all for you.

Oh listen, all you lovers of God, listen to what he did for me. I prayed, I begged, but with unceasing praises and absolute certainty that he would hear me. If he had detected the least false note, the least bit of hypocrisy in me, he would have turned a deaf ear—but no, the answer came, swift and sure, "I come!"

O blessed be God, who didn't ignore my pleas or stop loving me!

psalm 67

MAY GOD SHOWER HIS BLESSINGS UPON US, may he brighten our darkness with the sunshine of his smile so that everyone may know how good he is and how all salvation lies in him. Let everyone thank you, O Lord, let everyone give you thanks in abundance. Let all the nations of the earth break out into jubilant song because under you there will be true justice and inspired leadership. Yes, let everyone give thanks, every living being on the earth.

Look, look at the abundant harvest! Oh, may his blessings never, never end and may all four corners of the earth bow down before him in worship and adoration!

psalm
68

L ET GOD RAISE HIS HEAD that his enemies scatter wildly in all directions and those who dare hate him flee in a headlong rout. Let them vanish like smoke, melt away like bits of wax in a bonfire. *That* for all evildoers when he appears! But what have the just to fear? They are free to sing and dance for joy in his presence. So let them celebrate the Lord.

Sing, friends, rejoice, praise the Ruler of the heavens, for Lord is his name; laugh aloud in an ecstasy of exultation. No orphan, no widow needs to feel neglected, not with God as their protector, leaping to their aid from the heights of heaven. He shelters the homeless, breaks the shackles of those unjustly deprived of liberty. But rebels— the burning sands for them!

O God, with you leading us through the desert, things really happened! Earthquakes, torrential rains, even Mount Zion itself was rocked to its foundations at the presence of our God, the God of Israel. You broke the grip of the merciless drought that had held us in a stranglehold, revived us, close to despair.

Whole clans poured into the land, staking claims, settling their families and flocks. In your goodness you thought of everything, Lord, to ease the lot of the downtrodden. One word from you, O God, and victory was assured. The women, a great tidal wave of them, poured out of their houses shouting the glad tidings, "Victory! Victory! The enemy is routed, victory is ours, and there are rich spoils for all of us! Enough gold and silver to cover us from head to toe! Even those who merely sit and watch the flocks will be arrayed in finery." The wings of Israel, God's dove, will glitter and shimmer with fine worked gold and silver. And look there, the dead are piled as thick as snow on Mount Zalmon where God destroyed the enemy rulers.

Look at Bashan, mountain resplendent with towering peaks, magnificent, awesome. You rival mountain peaks, why so envious? Why look so green-eyed at the mountain God has chosen as his dwelling forever? Oh, this God of ours, see his approach, a magnificent procession! Tens of thousands of heavenly warriors in his escort, bearing him in their midst. His sanctuary is incomparably holy, transformed by his presence into another Sinai.

He moves majestically toward his abode on high; a vast throng of captives in tow testifies to his great triumph. Graciously he accepts the homage offered him, even the prostrations of the renegades are not spurned so that he can be truly Lord of all.

Oh blessed be God who comes to our aid day after day, stooping to bear our burdens himself—this God and Savior. And he has done this time and again, stepping between us and certain death, annihilating the enemy and casting their heads in the dust. "I'll hound them out of Bashan," he says, "scour the very bottom of the sea in my search so that you can have the pleasure of avenging yourselves on them, wading in their blood and providing a feast for your dogs."

What a procession! Awestruck, the multitudes gape at this victory march of my Lord and my God, shining with holiness and power, to his sanctuary. What color! What pageantry! Singers, musicians, and beautiful women striking golden cymbals and shouting, "Praise the Lord in the great assembly, bless him, you who have sprung from Israel's fountainhead!"

Look, there in front. Benjamin, the youngest, actually leading the procession. A leader. And there, the leaders of Judah forming a strong council, along with the leaders of Zebulun and Naphali bringing up the rear. God is your strength, O Israel. Yes, Lord, your power is always there for us; continue to mete out justice from your holy temple, where rulers come bearing tribute.

Rebuke Egypt, that hippopotamus sprawled in the reeds; rebuke these evil leaders and their still-worse progeny who resemble wild bulls and calves. Trample their bribes underfoot! Make short work of this brood of warmongers. Then Egyptian nobles will sue for peace, then Ethiopians will fall on their faces in adoration of the one God.

Break into song, O world! Sing his praises, O nations! This God, this Ancient of Days reigning from the heights of heaven. Listen, listen to the mighty voice of the Lord. Acknowledge his power, his complete authority over Israel. How awesome is this God in your midst, this God who shares his own power and strength with his people.

Blessed be he.

psalm

69

O GOD, I'M DROWNING—being sucked down into the quicksand of
misery. The waters of tribulation are about to close over me.
Hoarse and exhausted from hours of unanswered prayer, I strain my
eyes in search of some sign of relief, and—nothing. Look. Look!
More enemies than the hairs on my head, an array of them ready to
leap at my throat. Why? What have I done? Am I a thief? How can I
give back what I haven't stolen?

Dear God, I know I'm a fool, none of my imbecilities are a secret
to you. But please, don't let this be the cause of another's downfall.
Don't let them lose faith in you because of my suffering. Don't close
your ears to their prayers as you seem to have closed them to mine.
All of this happened to me because of my loyalty to you; I've completely lost face in the community because of you. Not even my own
brothers and sisters will own up to knowing me; they look right
through me and pass me by like total strangers—they! And we, born
of the same mother.

They've reduced me to tears of frustration by mocking at the
things of God and pouring contempt on me because of my steadfast
worship, because I'm consumed by my concern for the purity of your
temple, Lord. I fast, and they laugh at me; I put on sackcloth to howls
of derision. They talk me over on the street corners, tearing me apart;
even the town drunks get an audience because of the dirty songs
they've made up about me. But no, I continue, I go on pouring out
my prayers to you, Lord, ready and waiting for the moment when you
will once again be open to my entreaties. O God, out of your immea-
surable mercy give me living proof of the reality of your great power.

Rescue me from this quicksand relentlessly sucking me down,
down. Don't let me fall into the clutches of those who are trying to
drown me in miseries. Don't let life roll over me like a tidal wave,

dragging me down into the depths in total helplessness. Answer me, Lord, answer me, for pity's sake; your mercy and compassion are boundless. Don't look away, I need you desperately. Show them all how much I mean to you. You know the things they are charging me with, shameful, disgusting things—but I don't have to tell you, you can see for yourself.

They've broken my heart with their insults and contempt. I reached out for a helping hand, for understanding, for a kind word, but nothing. No one cares, no one listens. Instead, they rub it in, adding their poisonous hypocrisy to my already overflowing dish of suffering—like pouring vinegar down my raw parched throat.

I hope the same thing happens to them; I hope their fancy banquets are disasters and they and their fine friends belch until they strangle. May blindness close their prying eyes and searing pains pierce their guts, sapping all their strength. Come down on them, Lord, come down hard! Let them feel the full brunt of your rage. Drive them out of their cushy homes and turn their fine cities into ghost towns. They've got it coming for callously adding to the pain of someone you're purifying in the crucible of suffering.

They dare to vent their malice on one who is defenseless, weakened by the withdrawal of your favor and make public mockery of their victim's lot. May their consciences suddenly awake and give them no peace; may they be tortured day and night by bitter remorse; may they be driven to utter despair, cutting themselves off from all hope of forgiveness. Wipe them off your list, Lord, strike their names from the ranks of those you've chosen, those ordained for salvation.

But the pain, the pain, Lord, please make it stop. Help me to rise above all of them. Triumphant! And then! What songs, what praises, what acts of thanksgiving will pour out of me. This sacrifice of praise is more pleasing than all the offerings of money I could make to my Lord. All the so-called nobodies will have ample reason to rejoice; those who have worn themselves out in obedient and persevering worship in the darkness of faith will take heart. Yes, rejoice, friends, laugh. God is especially partial to the needy and those unjustly exiled for love of him.

Heaven, earth, sky, sea creatures—everything! Sing praise! God's coming to our rescue; Zion will be saved, I tell you; Judah rebuilt; and all of us will live there again, never to be dispossessed. Our own land! Ours to pass on to future generations, to all true worshipers of the one God.

psalm 70

HELP! GOD HELP ME! Oh please, come quickly! Shame these schemers who are after my blood; thwart their plans so carefully laid to undo me. Send them sprawling in complete disorder, let their mocking insults choke them.

But as for your friends, those who seek to love and serve you, may they know the exultation of being loved in return, the ecstasy of belonging heart and soul to you. May their greatest joy be in the singing of your praises, a jubilant and continuous cry of "Glory to God in the highest."

So I call to you, Lord, out of my wretchedness. Hurry, Lord, I need you. You are all I have, come soon, soon. . . .

LORD, I'VE PUT ALL MY TRUST IN YOU, don't let me endure disgrace in the very sight of those who are just waiting for my downfall. The innocent look confidently to you to rescue them from the clutches of the evil one because they know you are just. So listen to my plea, save me. Be a protecting wall around me, a secure place of refuge, a hiding place marked out for me from all eternity. O God, my rock—my fortress.

Save me, then, from the corrupt and ruthless; you're all I have left, my only hope. From as far back as I can remember, I've trusted in you, leaned on you from earliest childhood—you, who brought me safely from my mother's womb; you, whom I've praised continually. I know my suffering is an object of wonderment to many, but I stand unshaken in my faith in you. An unbroken stream of praise, honor, and love rises from me to heaven.

Dear God, I'm old now. You won't desert me will you? Don't leave me, now that old age is sapping my strength. My enemies are looking for an opening, they plot craftily, reveling in my waning powers, saying, "So? Fallible like the rest of us, huh? No special protection now. Well, watch every move and when the time is ripe—grab him! No one'll lift a finger to save that one."

Oh God, no, no, please come back to me, hurry for pity's sake, I need you. Cover them with disgrace and frustration so that their evil plans come to nothing. *That* for my enemies—exposure, condemnation!

But me? My hopes spring eternally, my praises only increase in intensity. All day long I'll broadcast your saving deeds, your wonderful justice, even though I can never exhaust the subject, try as I might. Arms upraised, I'll enter your sanctuary reciting a litany of your mighty deeds, the saving acts of the one God. O Lord, from earliest childhood what other teacher have I had but you? Even to this day there are fresh wonders to relate of your care. Don't stop loving me now that I'm old and grey, I still have so many wonders to set down for future generations to thrill to and profit by. Your power and your justice tower higher than the heavens themselves. Who is there to compare with you?

Oh my Beloved, you've cost me many bitter tears, it's true; but even if death overtake me, you would revive me and bring me up from the netherworld to resurrected life, giving me a crown of glory and filling me with joyful consolations. I'll play you a jubilant tune on my guitar, a song of thanksgiving plucked joyously on the strings once your promises are fulfilled, O Holy One of Israel. Yes, glad songs, shout-for-joy songs! It makes me so happy to praise you that my soul brims over with the sheer joy of it. The words and music simply pour out of me.

Every day, all day, I'll tell how you, in your justice, helped me, how fury consumes my disgraced and humiliated enemies.

O GOD, BLESS THE KING, and his son after him, with a share of your unerring justice. Then he will be a truly wise ruler, governing with firmness and seeing to it that the poor have their place in the sun. Peace and universal equity will crown the mountains and hills. The poor, the orphaned, the afflicted will flock to him for protection, while the unscrupulous will be ground into the dust. Holy fear and awe of you, O God, will stretch down through the ages, as lasting as the sun and the moon.

The king's bounty will embrace all, as rain covers thirsty meadows, and be received as showers falling on warm-turned earth. Then there will be a glorious reflowering of justice, and the blessings of peace will be unending. May his realm extend from horizon to horizon, from one end of the earth to the other.

Let the unruly and undisciplined bend their proud necks under his authority, let his enemies grovel in the dust. Why, rulers will come from afar, loaded down with tribute, from Tarshish, Sheba, and even Seba. All rulers and nations, in fact, will swear allegiance to him. And they will be treated to the sight of his openness to the pleas of the needy, his generosity to the poor; they will see what a friend he is to the friendless and helper to the helpless. He will be all compassion and pity where these are concerned. How precious their lives will be to him, how quickly he will leap to rescue them from the hands of those who would dare to oppress and victimize them.

God save the king!

May he receive gifts of finest gold from the mines of Sheba, and may blessings and prayers for him rise night and day. May the earth itself explode in homage with abundant wheat, an ocean of thick sheaves stretching right up to the mountain tops, rustling in the wind like the mighty cedars of Lebanon. And the cities—may they bustle happily with exultant throngs, a population as thick as the grass of the fields. May the king's name be held in such esteem that people bless themselves by it. May all nations acknowledge his blessedness.

Oh blessed be God, who alone can work such wonders. Blessings on his glorious name, may the whole world resound with his glories forever.

Book III

Psalms 73-89

psalm
73

OH THE GOODNESS OF GOD TO ISRAEL, to sincere hearts. But terrible to say, I came close to losing him, to an almost complete loss of faith. Envy was my undoing, envy of the callous and arrogant, who seem to have everything their way. They go through life hale and hardy, and in death they close their eyes in perfect peace, hands piously folded. Let other people be weighed down with troubles, not them. Let the rest of the world lose sleep over unpaid bills and problems of every kind, they're blissfully unconcerned. So of course they're proud as peacocks, looking down on the rest of us and ready to use violence to hold on to their elite positions.

Their eyes glitter with malice, snake eyes squinting glassily out of their fat faces. They give vent to their malicious thoughts in explosions of insults and blasphemies, ridiculing and vilifying others, uttering their denunciations with unbearable affectation and self-importance. They pass themselves off as prophets and with their pompous pronouncements usurp the authority of God himself. Of course their maxims spread like wildfire, as though they were veritable oracles. The poor gullible populace is taken in by them, they drink it all in. "After all," they say, "what do we really know about God? What's this wisdom, this omnipotence we hear of? How do we know it's true?" Yes, this is what these liars sink to, this is what they bring people to. And do you think they're punished for it? Hardly. They thrive and prosper.

Bitterness filled my heart as I mulled it over—"Have I been walking the straight and narrow for nothing? Is this what I get for my pains? It seems that all I get for all my trouble is more trouble. Every day a new installment of miseries."

But if I'd openly complained, Lord, imagine the bad example I'd have given to those who believe in you and who look to me for their lead. So I kept trying to understand what was happening to me and why, why, wrestling with this arduous problem to the point of exhaustion. Brain-weary I went to the temple, and as I prayed for light, I suddenly saw the link between here and hereafter.

Why of course, that's it—these malefactors are merely digging their own graves with each act of treachery they commit. Retribution? You're just giving them enough rope to hang them with in the end. Suddenly the noose will tighten and then . . . choking and blackness. All their glitter and celebrity will vanish like a dream as you turn on them in awesome reality and expose them for what they are. How stupid of me not to see this before; I let envy and bitterness blind me to the obvious. How pin-brained can you be? I was no better than a dumb ox.

But I could never really turn from you, we're too close, too intimately linked to ever be parted. You're guiding me, surely and directly, by divine inspiration, until in the end you'll welcome me into glory, arms wide open to receive me. What need do I have for anyone else with you at my side? No, there's no one, no one but you in the whole world. Even though I feel myself failing, what does that matter as long as I rest secure in your love? Those who desert you have only themselves to blame when things go wrong, for you leave them to their own devices and this means ruin. Just being near God is happiness enough for me; I'm totally dependent on him. All I want is to be allowed to spend the rest of my life telling the whole world how wonderful he is.

O GOD, WHY HAVE YOU CUT yourself off from us completely? Why are you so angry? What about the old days—what about all the love you lavished on us, building us up from next to nothing into a great nation, looked up to by everyone, you yourself making your home among us? And look at us now. Look at the ruins of your house—stripped to the walls. Oh please come before it's too late!

Bestial roars of triumph poured from within your sacred temple as they set up their own pagan banners in the sacred halls and over the entrances. Then their sacrilegious axe-wielding hands set to upon the priceless paneling, hacking it to bits like so many trees in a forest, raining blows left and right, destroying the work of a lifetime. And to complete the profanation, they put the battered remains to the torch, razing to the ground the dwelling sacred to your name. Every holy shrine suffered the same fate all over the country. "Come on," the enemy bellowed; "let's rid the land of them, once and for all!"

We've lost all sense of time and season, our prophets are struck dumb, unable to predict an end to this madness. Lord, tell us yourself when we can expect relief. Or are you going to let them mock you to your face forever? Why do you cloak your power? Reveal yourself and blast them into eternity!

Yet, I know full well, O my God, what you can do, what you have done in the past. You are still my God, as ever you were. And marvels? Why, you split the sea in two with one blow of your hand, making mincemeat out of the sea monsters cavorting in it. Leviathan's seven heads were scattered and beasts of prey fed on its carcass. Springs of water gushed forth at one word from you; flowing rivers dwindled to a trickle and dried up altogether at your will. Day and night, sun and moon, winter and summer—all, all under your complete control.

But keep in mind, Lord, what sort of people these are who attack you, how vile and low and despicable. Don't turn your chosen, helpless as turtle doves, over to them. Don't ignore us in our misery, we, your own family. Keep in mind the covenant we made, our commitment to one another. I tell you, every dark corner is alive with danger. Don't let them disperse your poor in fear and panic; no, give us cause to raise a song of thanksgiving and praise.

Lord! Your own honor is at stake, defend your good name. Don't ignore the torrent of abuse aimed at you by the hour. Don't close your ears to the sound of their taunts, it just eggs them on to greater outbursts of profanity.

O GOD, THANK YOU, THANK YOU. Your name is on every tongue as the tale of your wondrous intervention makes the rounds. It was just as you said:

"When the time is ripe, I myself will deal out justice in strict fairness. Just when everything seems on the point of collapse, I'll step in and breathe fresh life and vigor into them. Do you hear me, you smug know-it-alls? Well then, enough of your arrogance; and you, you hardened criminals, no more acts of ruthless terrorism. Stop showing off your muscle and crowing over your cheap conquests, you insolent blowhards."

Oh, I tell you, you can search east and west, desert and mountain, but God alone is the One who judges. He alone. One he wipes out, another he makes a mighty ruler. He holds a cup of retribution in his hand, foaming and deadly, and he'll ram it down the throats of the wicked.

But me? I'll never stop singing God's praises as long as I live. And I'll rid the earth of evildoers while giving the just their reward.

psalm
76

GOD IS FAMOUS IN JUDAH, his name a household word throughout Israel. He has established his abode among us, making Salem his home, the lair of the Lion of Judah. From this camp he sallied forth to defeat the enemy, shattering their shields and swords in fierce combat, frustrating their carefully laid strategies.

How wondrous you are, Lord, as you return in triumph from the battlefield, leaving it strewn with prey for the jackals. The bravest of the brave stripped of their powers, dead, all of them. Their strong arms useless to them now. One word from you rendered them powerless, they and their horses with them.

How fearsome you are, my God; in your power, who can withstand you? Your voice thunders from the heavens and the entire world cowers into trembling silence, dreading the judgment you are about to pass on those who terrorize the helpless.

The fury of human beings serves only to enhance your glory as you make playthings of their war machines; those who survive will be bound to your service.

Listen, all of you. Fulfill the vows you made in the hope of rescue. You neighboring nations come bearing gifts for this dread Lord who annihilates the powerful and before whom rulers grovel.

I SCREAMED AND CRIED TO GOD FOR HELP, I bellowed with all my might in the hope that God would hear me. In misery and bitterness I sought him, night after sleepless night; I sobbed out my soul, not allowing myself a moment of rest or a crumb of comfort. The thought of him cuts like a knife; dwelling on my problems brings me to the brink of despair.

Sleep is impossible, you've seen to that, and I haven't even the comfort of talking it over with anyone because words fail me completely. My life passes before my eyes and I see it all again, the old days when things were so right between us. I force myself to remember the songs, the happy times, brooding in the night, pondering long and hard: "So this is the end, is it? Is God finished with us? Are we completely and finally out of favor, tossed aside? Can we expect no more mercy, in spite of his repeated promises? What of his vaunted graciousness? Has he no more pity or compassion to spare, is he that angry? I think this is what crushes the most, the thought that he's changed, that he's no longer the Almighty One."

But no, all I have to do is dwell a bit more on all you've done in the past. Yes, Lord, on all the marvels you worked on our behalf. What wonders, what daring—my mind reels at the recollection of it all. O God, you're absolute perfection, absolutely other. Which of their gods can hold a candle to you? Your wonders are legendary, you've given marvelous demonstrations of your power among us. Single-handedly you saved your chosen people, we, the children of Jacob and Joseph.

The sea churned in terror at the sight of you, the subterranean depths rumbled and boiled. Torrential rains pelted the earth; ear-splitting thunder and blinding flashes of lightning struck terror. The seas parted convulsively, opening a path for you, and you sped through the walls of water so lightly that not a footprint remained to tell the tale. Shepherd-like, you led your people, entrusting them to the care of Moses and Aaron.

GATHER ROUND, FOLKS, BEND AN EAR; I've a lesson to teach and a tale to tell. Listen carefully because my message will be clothed in proverbs and tell of mysteries as I mull over the past and its meaning for our times. Everything we've heard, which has been passed down to us by our ancestors, we'll pass on to you, their descendants, revealing all to you, the younger generation—wondrous tales of the glorious things God has done—so that you too will sing his praises. God himself has laid it down as a sacred duty that these things will be passed on from parents to children, lest anything should be lost to posterity. He decreed that throughout all future generations children not even born yet would come to know of these wonders and pass them on to their children so that with full trust in God and always mindful of his achievements they would be faithful and obedient to his will. God forbid that they should act like their ancestors who proved to be such a proud and hardheaded lot, fickle and unfaithful to their promises.

The handpicked troops of Ephraim, expert bowmen, every one of them, deserted on the battlefield, turned tail and ran rather than own up to their obligations to God and the law. Everything he had ever done for them was forgotten in that headlong rout. What wonders he had performed before their ancestors' very eyes there in Egypt, in Zoan, the capital itself, making a safe path for them through the sea, the waters like glistening walls to right and left. By day a column of cloud led the way for them and at night it became a flaming torch illuminating their path. When they thirsted in the desert, water miraculously sprang up from sheer rock, shooting up as from some deep spring, swift running and crystal clear.

Do you think they were grateful? They showed what they were made of by brooding and grumbling among themselves against God, adding the sin of rebellion to all their other faults. Sulking because of their dwindling food supplies, they nursed resentment in their hearts and criticized God's leadership until it finally came to open complaint. "Why doesn't he give us something to eat? After all, if he can make water pour out of a rock, he should be able to come up with a little bread and a scrap of meat. Are we his people or not?"

Was God ever incensed over this! He was furious at Jacob, enraged at Israel for having so little faith and trust in him. Angrily he commanded the skies to open and manna literally rained down on them—they were knee-deep in it; fragrant sweet-tasting manna, fine enough for an angel to eat. And in such super abundance they collected it by the bushel. Not content with this, God spread his arms and winds sprang up from east and south and in a twinkling the sky was black with thousands of quail circling the camp and falling into their midst, the ground and the tents covered with them. Meat, meat, more than enough—more than anyone could possibly eat. The people fell upon them, gorging themselves on bird meat until they could hardly stand—this was the moment when God made them pay for their rebellion. Stomach pains attacked them, violent retching; the young and the strong, the most promising of them fell over, mowed down, doubled up in agony. They died before anything could be done for them.

Do you imagine that they learned anything from this bitter lesson? Incredible as it seems, they were worse then ever, adding loss of faith to all their other sins. So God made quick work of them, not one reached old age, and the years allotted to them a nightmare of wandering and fruitless toil. Whenever they were beaten in battle, they'd come crawling back to him on their hands and knees. Yes, all of a sudden they'd remember what he had done for them in the past;

now it was "Rock" and "Redeemer" again. Hypocrites. Lies, flattery, favor-seeking. They were as shallow and false as ever.

But he forgave them, again and again. He accepted their pleas and took them back because even though they could and did forget him, he couldn't and wouldn't forget them. He could have vented the full fury of his wrath upon them but he didn't; he held back because he was so mindful of their weakness, so compassionate toward their human frailty. Provocation after provocation they offered him on their journey through the desert, wounding his heart by their ingratitude and taunts, testing him, refusing to acknowledge his power over them. How easily they forgot all he had done, fighting their battles for them against the Egyptians, frightening the enemy into letting them go free by turning their drinking water into blood and sending swarms of flies and frogs to torment them. He devastated their fields with plagues of caterpillars, locusts, hailstones, and frosts, loosing all the forces of nature upon them, even wiping out their cherished flocks and herds. Wave upon wave of misfortunes swept over the land, scourges of God's anger, as epidemics raged out of control.

Finally, one terrible night, grim Death stalked the land leaving in its wake the dead bodies of all the firstborn, human and beast alike, from the palace of Pharaoh to the most miserable hovel. God's own people were spared; he led them safely through the carnage, as meek as lambs, and shepherded them through the desert—they were safe with him, they knew that—but their enemies, the sea swallowed up every one of them.

Surely, unerringly, he guided them to the frontiers of the promised land, to the very foothills of his holy mountain. Any pagans they came across he drove off, confiscating their land and possessions and turning everything over to his chosen ones.

Oh, if only they had shown a grain of gratitude. But again they failed him, turned against him, provoked him by giving themselves over to idol worship, building sacrilegious shrines and offering sacrifices to dead things. It was too much. They were as bad, if not worse than their ancestors. He exploded in hurt rage and disowned them completely, abandoning the holy dwelling. The ark and the people fell into the waiting hands of the enemy, and God didn't lift a finger to prevent the slaughter. Horror upon horror followed. The youngest and strongest among them were burnt at the stake, dooming the marriage hopes of many girls. Priests fought like soldiers and were cut down to a man, their widows struck dumb with grief.

But God could stand no more of it. Suddenly he was there again, springing into action with the reckless strength of a giant coming out of a drunken stupor. He came to the rescue of his people, sent all his enemies sprawling with one blow; they scattered in a headlong rout, defeated, broken.

He rejected Joseph, spurned Ephraim, and gave his love to Judah, to his beloved Mount Zion, seat of the sanctuary he built, beautiful as high heaven, firm as the everlasting earth. He looked about for a worthy steward and chose a simple shepherd boy, and gave his heart to David. God took him, a mere sheep-tender, and made him king. A shepherd was made shepherd of God's people, and David, being pure of heart, governed them wisely and well.

O GOD, WE'VE BEEN OVERRUN, invaded by foreigners. With bestial howls they've poured through the gates and into the Holy Place, polluting the very air with their pestilential presence. Jerusalem's been leveled to the ground and bodies are strewn everywhere for vultures and unclean dogs to feast on—it's been a horror, a bloodbath—because there isn't a soul left alive to bury them.

We're the laughingstock of the country, neighboring towns and cities mock us to our face, insults and abuse rain down on us from every side. How long do we have to bear this, Lord? Is there no end to your anger? Is your fiery jealousy to burn on forever, reducing us to smoldering cinders? It's them you should be angry with. They spurn you, utterly reject you. And look at how they've abused us, look at the murder and looting!

Please, don't hold the failures of our ancestors against us, help us for pity's sake, we're in desperate straits. Add luster to your holy name by coming to our rescue, save us, forgive us. Why give our enemies the satisfaction of saying, "Where's their mighty God now?" Show them what happens to those who dare spill the blood of your friends and intimates. Give us the joy of witnessing their utter terror.

Open your ears to the sighs and groans of those unjustly imprisoned, stay the hand of the executioners. Pay the enemy back sevenfold for daring to doubt your sovereign power. Then we, your children, will split the air with our songs of praise and thanksgiving, triumphant hymns that will ring down through the ages.

psalm

80

O GOD, O SHEPHERD, O Leader of Israel, listen to us, please. Lean down from your glorious throne on high and display your dazzling splendor before Ephraim, Benjamin, and Manasseh. Marshal your forces and speed to our rescue. Restore us to your good graces, the graces that will insure a secure future for us.

How long are you going to nurse this anger of yours toward us, turning a deaf ear to our cries of distress? Our bread is soaked with our tears; yes, we wash down our food with them. We're fought over by our covetous neighbors, haggled over, all seizing as much as they can grab, laughing in our faces all the while. Take us back, O God, so that we can look forward to an end to these tortures.

Have you forgotten that you yourself transplanted us from Egypt as carefully as a choice vine, driving away all other peoples in order to make room for us? In fertile soil we took root and quickly blossomed in such rich profusion that we settled the entire country, from the southernmost mountains to the forests of the north, and from the western sea to the Euphrates in the east.

Then who can understand this sudden reversal of fortune, this unlooked-for breaching of our borders, so that we're exposed to invasion on every side? Our enemies are free to devour us with the ferocity of wild beasts. Oh, turn back to us Lord, cast your eyes in our direction and see what has become of your handiwork, the fruit of your planting, to the precious heir, so carefully nurtured and protected. This pampered plant is put to the torch and hacked to bits; cut off from your favor, it withers and dies. Cup your protecting hands over the people, over those you created to give you glory. Never again will we show disloyalty, we swear it. Put new heart into us and we'll shout our allegiance from the housetops.

O Lord, our God, if you take us back into your good graces, our salvation is assured.

S ING GLAD SONGS TO OUR STRONG HOLY GOD, shout it out for the God of Jacob. Play joyously on stringed instruments. Serenade, rhapsodize, as the moon casts its silvery light over our festivities. God himself has established this festival, declaring it to be a perpetual day of jubilation in commemoration of Israel's liberation from Egypt.

But wait, what's this I hear? Whose voice is that? "I'm the One who took the heavy load off your back, the One who plucked the bulging work basket out of your hands. I who heard your groans and wailing and came to your rescue. I was there in the midst of your suffering, for it was I who tested your love at Meribah. It was all my doing. Now listen to me (oh, why won't you listen?) let me warn you. There's to be no idol worship among you. None, do you hear? Bow to no foreign god. I'm your God, your Lord God, who led you out of cruel Egyptian captivity. I, who am divinely capable of giving you anything you want, just for the asking.

"But they wouldn't listen to me; my people didn't pay the least attention to my words, wanted no part of me. So I threw up my hands in disgust and abandoned them to their own devices. A little good will, a willingness to follow my lead and their troubles would be over like that. I'd wipe out everyone who opposes them, turn from punishing Israel to exterminating their enemies. What they're missing! Their ruthless enemies, haters of God, would all grovel in the dust at their feet—never would I relent; no, their sentence would be irrevocable. And, oh, how I would delight in spoiling my darling Israel, spoon-feeding every one of them with honeyed wheat."

G OD, THE SUPREME JUDGE, stands in judgment on the judges saying, "Enough of making a mockery of justice! Enough of wink-
ing at the sins of the influential and powerful! You seem to have
forgotten that your job is to defend the defenseless, befriend the
friendless, and shelter the orphaned. You're to give a fair hearing to
the penniless and provide for the poor and victimized."

Bah! Ignoramuses, the lot of them; blind as bats, they undermine
the very structures of human society by their corruption.

"Listen to me, your calling was holy, a vocation given you from
on high, a sharing in my own authority. Well, don't think that your
influential positions will save you; you'll suffer the same fate as all
sinners do, and you'll be twice as culpable! If I don't spare princes,
do you think you'll fare any better?"

Yes, Almighty God, you yourself be our Judge, not just over Israel
but over the entire world. After all, you own it all, hold it in the palm
of your hand.

psalm
83

WHY SO SILENT, GOD, why this void? Don't be so unconcerned, so unresponsive. I tell you, your enemies are raising an uproar, they're massing for an attack!

They burn the midnight oil in all-night war councils, mapping out their strategy against us, your own people. "Come on," they hiss, "divide and conquer, wipe them off the face of the earth." For once, they're united in their unholy alliance and it's you—yes, you—who are the real target. From all over they come, a vast sea of multicolored tents representing Edom, the Ismaelites, Moab, and the Hagarites; look out there, the tents of Gebal, Ammon, and Amalek, and Philistia and Tyre have come too. O God, even dread Assyria has lent its strength to the campaign.

Come down on them, Lord, do what you did at Midian, doom them to the same fate as Sisera, as Jabin suffered at the river Kishon. What a slaughter that was—their rotting corpses left to manure the ground. Cut down their rulers and generals like all those who boasted they would conquer and possess God's own land. Descend on them like a tornado, consume them like a raging fire consumes and devours entire mountainsides. Unleash all the forces of nature against them, humble them to the ground so that they'll be forced to acknowledge your might and beg for mercy.

May they never know anything but shame, disgrace, and annihilation. It's the only way they'll ever know that you alone are Lord, Master of the universe.

psalm 84

HOW BEAUTIFUL YOUR HOUSE IS, LORD, how beautiful. How long I've waited and desired with all my soul to stroll along the marble courts of my God.

My heart is ablaze with desire for God, I can feel it in the very marrow of my bones. Just as birds unerringly wing home to build nests for their young, so I find my resting place nestled by your altars, my Lord and my God.

Oh to be among those who actually live there, free to spend every hour singing your praises. How blessed they are to confess with their whole being that their strength does indeed come from the Lord and to keep their hearts always turned toward his Temple—a perpetual spiritual pilgrimage.

Just by their irrepressible joy, pilgrims transform the most barren landscapes into gardens; even the very heavens collaborate by sending thirst-quenching rains. They thrive on the rigors of travel, getting stronger as they approach the holy city; there's not one who fails to reach the desired goal.

Hear my prayer, O God—bless your anointed, O God, our Protector, and keep us ever in your sight, for one day with you is far more blessed than a thousand without you. And I would rather be a helpless beggar at your threshold than the guest of honor at the banquets of the ungodly.

God is everything to me—sun, shield, grace, glory—for he lavishes himself on those who are true to him. Oh my God, how blessed the lot of those who trust only in you.

S AFE AGAIN, SAVED BY THE HAND OF THE LORD! Our land has been blessed and our fortunes have revived. All our sins have been forgiven, wiped out, forgotten. O blessed Lord, you're not angry with us anymore, your explosive wrath has finally cooled. Hallelujah!

Make your forgiveness complete by restoring us fully to your favor, by a real show of friendship. Or is your displeasure going to simmer on forever? Why not wipe the slate clean instead, restore our hopes, and give your people double cause for celebration? Be good to us, Lord; please Lord, put us once more under your sure protection.

Wait, listen, he's speaking. He's going to grant peace to his people, to those who are faithful (but disaster for them if they return to their wicked ways).

How lovingly he protects those who draw near to him with fitting awe and reverence. His glorious Presence will dwell in our midst once more. With him amongst us Mercy and Truth are one, Justice and Peace seal their love with a kiss, Truth reaches up to heaven where Justice awaits with open arms. God himself will distribute gifts aplenty, and our land will abound with rich crops.

Justice will pave the way before him and Salvation follow in his wake.

86

LISTEN TO ME, PLEASE LORD, give me a hearing; I'm poor and in deep trouble. Give me your protection; I'm your friend, I trust you, rely on you completely. Be good to me; I cry out to you day and night. A word, my God, all I ask is a word of encouragement to give me some hope. The eyes of my soul are trained on you constantly.

I know how good you are, how you forgive and forget, showering kindnesses on all who ask for your help. So listen to me now, be open to my petition. I know who to turn to when trouble comes. Truly, there's no one like you; none of their little tin gods can compare with you, no marvels equal those you perform—my God, the things you do. The whole world lies at your feet in adoration, for you made it, created it from scratch to give you glory—you who are incomparably great, infinitely creative, the one God.

I want to learn to follow you; teach me, please, so I can be honest and true, simply filled with the wonder of you. Then I'll make the heavens resound with my loud praises, my shouts of thanksgiving; I'll be the living personification of your mercy and power to save. How good you've been to me—so much love. But Lord, there's a conspiracy against me, proud and arrogant people have formed an unholy alliance to bring me down; they're without shame or fear of divine retribution. What a contrast with you, my God, who are full of love and compassion, so patient, so ready to forgive. I ask you, please, as one of your very own household, give me strength. Show them I've got a powerful Friend who truly cares for me. Imagine their shame and confusion when they see me safe and happy in spite of their schemes.

psalm 87

G OD'S OWN CITY STANDS SHINING on top of his holy mountain. Truly, Zion is more precious to him than all the other cities of Jacob put together.

How world famous you are, O city of God, the things they say about you, such glorious praises. God himself exults: "Rahab and Babylon, my conquests, along with my other victories, Philistia, Tyre, and Ethiopia, will be reborn in Zion—adopted as native children. 'Why, they were born here,' people will say."

All nations that stream toward Zion will be given the right to boast, "We belong here," because Zion's motherhood is a universal motherhood by God's decree. And when God takes the roll call of his people, he'll say of each and every one, "Yes, a born Israelite."

Whether they sing or dance for joy, their one thought will be "I belong!"

psalm

88

O GOD, MY CRIES OF DISTRESS rise up to you morning and night. Please, won't you listen, won't you answer? I've had my fill of misery, and death is staring me in the face. I already feel tried, judged, and condemned, limp with dread and apprehension. No—worse still —I feel already dead and buried in an unmarked grave, forgotten by God and humans . . . down, down, at the bottom of a black pit.

Your anger has pulverized me, and I'm all alone, cut off from everyone who knows me, like a stinking leper. And I'm powerless to do anything about it, that's the most horrible part. Blinded by tears, I raise unseeing eyes toward you, my hands held high in mute supplication, hoping for rescue before it's too late.

Aeieii—what can you expect from someone dead, Lord? Can ghosts sing your praises or offer you thanks? Is the grave a sign of your clemency, or a rotting corpse evidence of your loyalty? And how, in the name of all that's holy, can the news of your marvels be told in that dark and dreadful country of the dead? What ray of light could ever come from that place?

No matter. While I still have the breath of life in me, I'll continue to storm heaven for mercy. But why have you done this to me? Why this rejection, why this back unyieldingly turned on me? All I've ever known from the cradle is trouble and misery, double my share of horrors at your hand. My mind reels with the reality of it all. I'm scorched by the hot blasts of your anger, finished—done for— drowned like a rat in this sea of calamities. Not a friend, not a neighbor left, you've seen to that too—everything I held dear swallowed by blackness.

psalm
89

OUR LOVE WILL BE LIKE A SONG FOREVER, dear Lord, beautiful music down through the ages. I have always said this mercy of yours is eternal, made in heaven itself. And you?

"I have made a solemn bond with my chosen one. I have given David my sworn word, 'I promise you that your name will live on forever, never will your house fall.'"

The heavens will explode with joy, the vast angelic army thrill with the wonder of it all. What deity could hold a candle to you, O God, what heavenly body could even come close to you in dazzling splendor? Why, when God holds court, the entire cosmos bows down in awe and wonder. Lord God Almighty, where is there strength to equal yours? Your fidelity radiates from you in all directions, bathing everything in shimmering light. The mighty oceans are your play-things and at your command the crashing waves shudder and lie still. You have squeezed the life out of arrogant Rahab and sent all your enemies sprawling with one sweep of your hand.

The heavens, the earth, the entire universe—all creation belongs to you who made it all. The world from horizon to horizon, your masterpiece—Mounts Tabor and Hermon rumble joyously in praise of you. What strength in your arms, what power in your hands, those awesome hands. Your throne rests on the strong pillars of Justice and Integrity. Goodness and Truth form a highway before you. What joy for those attuned to your voice, O Lord, they revel in the sunshine of your favor. Your name is a celebration day by day, your justice a cause for national pride. For you are our greatest boast and it is thanks to you that we are raised to such lofty heights. God is our protector, God is Israel's King!

Once, in a vision, you made a great revelation through your prophet, "It is my pleasure to appoint a leader from among the people, one of the strongest among them. I have discovered David, he truly serves me. I have decreed that he be anointed with my Spirit so that he will be supported by my own hand forever and my own strength will pour through him to make him invincible. No enemy will ever outwit him, no malefactor ever bring him to grief. I will deal personally with his enemies and all who hate him will pay heavily. He will enjoy my continual favor, and because he is mine, everything he sets his hand to will succeed. He will straddle the world like a giant, master over the rivers and the seas. He will offer me true praise, and call to me, 'My Father, my God, my Stronghold.'

"Wherever he goes, the first place will be his, with all the rights of the royal firstborn. My mercy will protect him, my sworn word stand by him, unshaken. His posterity will stretch down through the ages in an unbroken line, never will his house or throne lack an heir. But—be warned—should any of his sons break faith with me, becoming willful and disobedient; if they turn a deaf ear to me, and my commandments, becoming a law to themselves, I will be forced to make an example of them. Yet, I will not hold David responsible or withdraw my love from him. I will not retract the oath I have made; once having promised, nothing can make me go back on my word. His family will endure, his throne will stand, as immovable as the sun in its sky and the moon in its orbit."

But—what is this, Lord? Everything has gone wrong. You have turned on David's descendant, you have rejected him—the bond is broken, the house destroyed, his crown rolled in the dust. All his walls breached, all his defenses down, prey to every passing marauder, mocked at and ridiculed by his neighbors. His enemies win ridiculously easy victories over him as if you were on their side now. Such gloating, such raucous guffawing over your fallen servant. The former glory of David's house is a thing of the past, it lies, buried under tons of rubble. A mere boy when he came to power, his reign is pitifully short-lived; disgrace is all he knows now.

Tell us how long this dreadful situation is to last, Lord. When can we look for some cooling of your anger? Is it going to rage forever? Life is so short, are we to end our days in emptiness and frustration? Everyone has to die sooner or later, we know that; death has no favorites.

But what about all your promises? Where are all your blessings now? And the promises, vows, made to David our ancestor, what about them? You have only to listen to the insults leveled at us to know the depths to which we have fallen. I bear within myself the entire burden of the curses showered down upon us, the curses which pursue and dog our footsteps, the footsteps of your chosen ones.

Still . . .

Blessed be the Lord God forever.

Amen and Amen.

Book IV

Psalms 90-106

O GOD, YOU'VE CARRIED US in your arms throughout the ages, you who existed before the mighty mountains, who are God before ever turning your mind to the creation of the earth or the whole universe itself. From infinity to infinity, you are. A word and you return human beings to the dust you took them from, for what is time to you? A thousand years but a flicker of an eyelash. And humans, what are they? Like sand of the shore that is washed into the sea, a dream-like existence at best. A human being's existence is as lasting as scrub grass that shoots up in a day and lies scorched and limp from the sun by nightfall—useless.

But you, Lord, how awesome you are, how devastating your anger. It leaves us spent and gasping, paralyzed by the fear of annihilation. You've unmasked us, laid bare our heinous sins, all those shameful degrading things we thought no one would ever know about. We never reckoned with your all-seeing eyes. So our days wend their leaden way under the blast of your wrath, and our lives wind down with a weary groan. How much time can anyone expect to live, after all? Seventy years? Maybe eighty, if we're strong. And for what? A lifetime of fruitless toil and frustration, then it's over and we're gone. Is there any understanding you? Any gauging the full extent of your terrible powers? Fear of the Lord only comes with the experience of your fury. Help us to really grasp the brevity of life so that we will grow in wisdom.

Please, Lord, come back to us. Please relent and be merciful. Grant us a fresh new start. What a difference it would make to be able to hope again, to be happy again. Let our joy mount as high as our misery brought us low, let us see clearly—your hand in all that has happened to us, your will gloriously evident. May your blessings rain down on us and may everything we attempt win approval, yes, everything.

psalm

91

L ISTEN TO ME, all you who rest upon the heart of God and lie
hidden in the shadow of the Almighty. You are the ones who
will always say to him, "My defender and refuge, my God, I trust
you completely."

Yes, trust him. He can save you from any danger, any trap laid
out to ensnare you and bring you to a violent end. Protectingly, he
will spread his wings over you, there you will be safe. He has promised it and his word stands before you like an impregnable wall.

No need to fear the sudden nightly ambush or the brazen assault
by light of day, the fever that rages in the night or the sun that blisters
at high noon. Even if the world collapses around you, the death toll
in the thousands to your right and left, you'll remain unscathed, and
witness with your own eyes what becomes of unregenerate sinners.

And all this because God is your sure refuge. Yes, you have wisely
made the Most High your home and dwell there, firmly rooted in
God. Nothing can touch you now, no sickness undermine your
health. Your every move will be watched over by angels, their hands
ready to snatch you out of every danger, not allowing you to even
stub your toe. Scorpions and lions will be so much dirt under your
feet for you to trample on and grind into the dust.

I know how they really love me, and so, what can I do but respond with a like love, putting them under my special protection. I
will raise them above all others, safely out of reach of their enemies
because they offer me real worship and heed me like obedient children. I will answer all their prayers, they have only to ask. In any
distress I will be there to rescue them and so give them honor in the
sight of all. They will enjoy a long happy life; I will reveal all my secrets to them and they will know how I manage human affairs, providing for every need in my wisdom.

HOW SOUL-SATISFYING IT IS to have a grateful heart, Lord, to sing your praises, O Mighty One. To wake up singing divine love songs, and strum the story of your fidelity on stringed instruments through the night. You've made me so proud, so happy because of the things you do—I have to shout it out! What marvels, what depth of thought—completely beyond the crass and ignorant, non-existent to the brute fool. Sinners may abound like poisonous mushrooms and criminals proliferate like weeds, but only so their sudden annihilation can give greater glory to you, O God the All-Powerful.

Your enemies, Lord, your scheming enemies, will be wiped out, every one of them. Their ranks broken up and all of them scattered in headlong flight. Then, oh then, my time will come at last—vindication, honors, the victor's gladness. Best of all, I'll have the satisfaction of seeing my persecutors get what's coming to them. The joy of it all—their howls of anguish will be music to my ears.

Mark my words, there's a bright future for the honest; they can stand tall and proud, sure of constant progress in every virtue and endeavor. Old age won't diminish the fruitfulness or sap the strength of the upright, their sturdiness and vigor will be clear evidence of God's work in them. They'll give true glory to God, my rock, in whom there could never be a speck of evil.

93

GOD IS SUPREME! Majesty adorns him, strength cloaks him; he strapped it on like a massive belt, and everything fell into place —the world firmly fixed in the cosmos. Your sovereignty immovably established from that moment, O Lord, until time is no more.

Calamities may surge around us like tidal waves, the sound a deafening roar drowning out everything else, forcing everything from our consciousness. Yet, greater than any storm of trouble, greater than any horrors that hover over us, horrors poised and ready to annihilate us, is God—all-powerful, all-high, all-holy.

Your laws are eternal, my God, your sacred house will be adorned with holiness to the end of the ages.

GOD OF VENGEANCE, where are you? God of vengeance, make your presence felt! Show your strength, give the accursed proud what they've got coming! How long are these miserable bloodsuckers going to have it their way? How long are they going to stand over us, gloating, pouring out floods of profanity?

They keep your people in a state of perpetual turmoil, victimizing widows and orphans, murdering the defenseless. And they taunt us to our faces, "Pah! this God of yours knows nothing! He's blind or just doesn't care *that* about you."

Well, listen to this, you dumb brutes; yes, I mean you, you dull-witted fools. When will you ever learn? Do you think that the God who could make the wonder of a human ear could be deaf? Who fashioned the miracle of the human eye could be blind? Who wipes out entire nations with a sweep of his hand would hesitate to deal out well-earned punishment—this God who's the fount of all knowledge? You can be sure of this, he knows all our thoughts, just how empty they are.

O Lord, what a blessing it is to have you for a teacher, to receive the law from your very lips. The law that upholds human beings and consoles them when troubles abound, a sure sign that the wicked will come to a bad end—are on their way even now into the black pit. Could God ever abandon his people totally? No, all will be well and with light hearts the people will know the joy of right-living.

Who else but my God would stand up for me, who else would take my part in the fight against my evil enemies? If he hadn't come to the rescue, it would have been all over for me. Whenever I feel myself slipping, I can feel you near, loving me, supporting me, Lord. In the midst of turmoil you soothe and calm me, flooding my soul with light and peace.

Corrupt judges, who twist and pervert the law, had better not count on your help. They don't speak or act in your name. How could they, smiling at perjury and condemning the innocent to death? But I can be sure of protection and refuge in God, while all they can expect is what they've brought down on their own heads, God's iron hand crashing down.

They'll pay for their crimes—they'll be wiped off the face of the earth. God will see to it.

COME ON EVERYBODY, SING! Shout for joy to God our Savior! Let's show our gratitude in happy, bubbling-over-with-joy songs. Because he's an incomparable, tremendous Lord, greater than all the others put together. The whole world, from the deepest of deeps, to the highest of heights is his creation alone, and so are the rolling oceans and endless deserts.

So come on, down on your knees! Faces in the dust! Let's worship the Lord our Maker, for he is ours and we are just little sheep in his pasture. Like good sheep we must listen to the voice of our Shepherd, calling, "Don't close your hearts to me as your forebears did back there in the desert at Meribah, and on that terrible day in the wilderness of Masseh when they dared to defy me—question me after all I'd done for them!

"I put up with them for forty long years of anger and frustration, until finally I threw up my hands in disgust, 'They're stupid as well as fickle, incorrigible every one of them.' And I made up my mind, then and there, that never, ever, would I accept them."

psalm 96

OFFER FRESH OUTPOURINGS OF SONG TO GOD, sing his praises—sing, sing! Sing, all you peoples of the earth! Make music, melodious song, bless him endlessly, tell everyone you meet the joyful account of our deliverance. Be an apostle of praise, proclaim his works far and wide. For surely God is great and so greatly to be praised. He is fearsome and awe inspiring, infinitely more than all other gods. What are these other gods anyway? Why, it's our God who created the heavens themselves. Majesty and glory radiate from him, strength and beauty are like mighty pillars in his temple.

Come on, don't hesitate, everyone's invited to sing his praises, the entire human family urged to give glory to his power and strength. We owe it to him, he deserves it! So come on, gather up the best offerings and join the happy throng, the jubilant procession winding its way up to his courts. Let your good deeds praise him, too, adorn yourselves in virtue like splendid festive robes. Fling yourselves on your faces in awe and trembling.

Shout out the news of God's reign to all the world, tell them all that the future of the earth is secured, nothing can ever uproot it. And he will deal fairly with everyone, all will receive their due. Be glad, heavens, jubilate earth, roar with delight, seas and oceans. And you fields and meadows, with all your creeping and crawling and hopping things, jump for joy. Join voices in a welcoming anthem, you towering trees of the forest. He comes—he comes to rule us justly!

psalm 97

GOD IS ENTHRONED; be glad, O world. And all you little islands sing with joy. How awesome he is, his cloak like a dark luminous cloud about him, his throne immovably rooted in fairness and justice. Fiery tongues of flame announce his approach, incinerating his enemies on every side. Lightning bolts turn night into day, sending tremors of fear through the earth. Even mighty mountains collapse in dismay, melting away like wax from the sheer terror of this dread Lord of creation. But the heavens explode into shouts of praise; his glory is laid bare for all to marvel at.

Dishonor on those given to idol worship! Imagine, taking pride in a dead pile of stones—as if they had any power to save. Why, all these gods grovel in the dust before him, all toppled from their lofty perches. What welcome news this was to Zion; what cause for celebration in Judah, this fresh proof of your wisdom, O Lord, O Greatness, O Infinity. Infinitely beyond their little stone gods.

Friends of God, abhor sin, avoid it at all costs. God watches over his own, protecting them and snatching them out of harm's way. They're never out of his sight. He floods their souls with light and fills their hearts to bursting with joy.

So be glad in him, you pure of heart, and thank him—thank him endlessly.

98

L ET'S RENEW OUR PRAISES OF GOD; he's done it again! Single-handedly and by his own strength he's won the day. And so he's revealed his might, a wondrous display, dazzling all who see it. He's been faithful to his word to Israel, showing unbounded mercy; now the whole world knows the story.

Break into happy song, world, shout for joy, jubilate! Strum your guitars, make music. Blow your silver trumpets in an ecstasy of joy, fill the air with beautiful song, a tribute to the Lord. Roar with exultant praise, you oceans, cry out you creatures of the deep, and you, too, earth, along with everything that moves upon you.

Applaud, you crashing ocean waves; sing, you sky-scraping mountains, sing songs of welcome as he comes in triumph. For surely, he comes to reign in complete fairness, in truth and justice, over us.

G OD SITS ENTHRONED and everyone is awestruck at the sight; myr-
iads of angels bear him—tremble, earth. How great his power
over Zion, how complete his mastery over the world. Let them show
gratitude, for, O! how holy you are!

O Lord, you are in love with justice and fairness, basing all your
actions on our behalf upon them. Worship him, Jacob, down on your
knees, faces in the dust, for truly he is the Holy One.

Moses and Aaron were handpicked by the Lord, Samuel too, and
he spoke at their bidding, his voice echoing mysteriously from within
the pillar of cloud. They obeyed him to the letter. How often, Lord,
you answered their pleas; time and again you pardoned your people,
but true to yourself, you also handed out well-deserved punishment.

So exalt the Lord our God, come on your knees to his holy mountain to do him homage, for the Lord our God is worthy of it.

MAKE MELODY TO THE LORD, peoples of the world; let's have a joyful outpouring of song. Serve him gladly, willingly, eagerly; dance into his presence for sheer joy. Never forget that this is God Almighty—he made us from nothing, we didn't spring into existence on our own—we are his creation, his people, his flock.

When you enter his presence bring a grateful heart, a happy heart, a song-filled heart. Thank and praise him for everything he's done.

Oh, how good he is, how inexhaustible his mercy, how undying his love!

psalm
101

L ORD, I WANT TO RHAPSODIZE about your love and mercy; listen to my song of praise. I've reformed, Lord, truly I have. When can I hope to see you? My house is worthy of you now, Lord, all is peace and goodwill. I've turned my back on my old ways and make quick work of any underhanded bid to tempt me from the straight and narrow. No more traffic with hypocrites and scandalmongers, no more rubbing elbows with the proud and arrogant.

No, my friends now are the kindly and God-fearing, my door is wide open to the honest and upright; these are my intimate associates from now on. Liars, look out! Hypocrites, steer clear! The light of day will show them up for what they are and that will be the end of them.

psalm
102

L ORD, LISTEN TO ME, be open to my pleading. Don't turn away, please, just when I need you most. I need your help, I need it now! My life's going up in smoke, my bones are on fire. Misery has made me even forget to eat, I'm wasting away—my skin hangs in folds like a pelican's and I hoot like a mournful owl in the desert. Sleep's impossible, I toss and turn endlessly; I feel as alone as a sparrow perched on a housetop.

On top of all this I've got to bear the insults and mockery of my gloating enemies. They spit out my name like a curse, using it like a stick to beat me with. Everything has the taste of ashes, everything's drowned in bitter tears. And all of this the result of your anger. We were like one but you've thrown me aside, and the future looms darker and darker, my prospects like so much sun-scorched grass.

Still, I've one consolation—you can never change or be dethroned, through all the endless ages your memory can never be effaced. And so, I'm certain that you'll take pity on Zion one day, a day that seems to be coming, all signs point to it. Zion, precious ruin—how we love it! Every stone of it; even its dust moves us to tears.

Once again the watching nations will be struck with awe at the sound of your name, O God, their rulers will prostrate before your glory. When Zion rises from the dust, God will be revealed in all his splendor. He'll answer our prayers and not abandon us to our fate; everything will be carefully recorded for posterity, so that not one deed is lost, so that unborn generations will have abundant cause to praise him. They'll know that he heard our prayers and saved us from extinction. His praises will ring in Zion, in Jerusalem, wherever the people gather to offer him worship.

And me? I barely crawl through life; he's sucked all the strength out of me, my end is near. It's too soon, Lord. Why cut off my poor life when yours is endless? Before time ever was, you were busy laying out the foundations of the earth and salting the heavens with stars. And even when they're all gone, you'll still be. The earth, the sun, the moon, and the stars will disappear one day, shrugged off like worn out clothing, but not you, never you—you are. You are the Lord. Your chosen ones will share in all this, their line will be unending, like you.

M Y SOUL, BLESS THE LORD; bless him, every fiber of my being. My soul, praise the Lord and never forget everything he's done for you. Your sins, your many sins, forgiven; your body, sound and made strong again. Rescued from death time and again and showered with consolations. His goodness follows you into old age, filling you with youthful vigor, like the ageless eagle.

The downtrodden have only to call upon God to receive a fair hearing. Moses was his special friend and God spoke to the people through him. How merciful and loving God is, ever patient and ever ready to forgive. He's not one to be forever scolding nor does his anger fume on endlessly. He's never given us what we really deserve for our sins or vented the full force of his justified wrath on our heads.

Measure the sky, if you can, and you'll have a little idea of just how big his love is for those who honor him. As far as east is from west, that's the distance he puts between us and our sins. Like a kind father, he understands our weaknesses and knows we're only handfuls of dust after all. Human life, what's that? Human beings are no more lasting than wildflowers. Lovely today, and tomorrow? . . . blown away, forgotten. But the love of God—that's endless. It reaches out to us down through the ages, from parents to children, parents to children, warming and preserving those who love him in an unbroken stream into infinity, those who are docile and obedient.

You bright angels, obedience personified, all you heavenly choirs, who leap to accomplish his slightest desire, praise him, bless him. World, cosmos, everything created by his hand, adore him.

Bless the Lord, O my soul!

COME, MY SOUL, let's praise the Lord. O my God, what greatness is yours. Majesty and glory are draped around you like shining garments and light envelops you like a brilliant cloak. You've flung the starry heavens over us like a billowing tent, your royal palace is balanced upon the sparkling heavenly waters. You make the flying clouds a chariot, streaking across the skies on wings of the wind, and harness the mighty gales to carry out your designs; darting flames leap and skip at your word.

You've secured the earth firmly in its orbit, never to be displaced, and cloaked it in vast blue oceans. The waters stood higher than the mountain tops, but one flash of your eyes and they retreated in a rush, one mighty roar of your voice, and they tumbled over one another as they plunged to their fixed depths. Your voice rolled over the waters, setting up boundaries never to be breached, so that never again can they cover the earth and bury it. Springs bubble up in the valleys, winding their way among the hills, quenching the thirst of the wild beasts and the wild asses who drink their fill; along the streams leafy trees grow filled with singing birds.

Cloudbursts drench the hillsides, vegetation fairly explodes from the earth—lush green grasses for the cattle, heavy yields of fruit and grain for human beings, a reward for their work, providing bread and nourishment for their tables. Enough wine to gladden anyone's heart, oil to set the face glistening, soul-satisfying stores of bread.

The Lord's trees, his mighty cedars, are set in well-watered soil; there are singing birds on every branch and storks nest happily among the boughs of the lofty evergreens. Every creature has a place to call its own; mountain sides for goats, cliffs for rock hyraxes—how right it all is.

Lord, you've thought of everything. The moon to tell us the seasons, the sun the time of day. At your word darkness falls, and now it's time for the beasts of the night to steal out, as though by signal, to seek their prey. Their hungry roaring says, "Give us food, Lord! Feed us too!" Then at the first streaks of dawn they slip back to their lairs, sated with meat, to rest from the hunt. And now, it's people who come out to their set tasks, toiling from sunrise to sunset.

How innumerable your works, O Lord, how great your wisdom, how beautiful your handiwork. The whole world's a testament to them. Just look at the sea, so vast and tumultuous, full of every conceivable creature, of every conceivable size. Great ships sail across it, huge whales sport in it; and all of them, human and beast alike, are totally dependent upon you for their food. Openhandedly you distribute your gifts, eagerly they gather them up. But when you close your hand, distress grips everything—when you withdraw life-giving breath, they all are reduced to dust. Again, you send your Spirit and fresh life springs up and the earth's made new again.

God's glory is never-ending, he takes unceasing pleasure in his creation; but with one look he can destroy it all, shaking the earth to its foundations, sending the mountains up in smoke. I want to spend the rest of my life praising him, making music for him as long as there's breath in my body. How sweet the thought of him is. He is my joy.

Enough of sinners—away with them. Let my soul's cry be hallelujah!

G IVE THANKS TO GOD, call out to him, shout his name, tell everyone all about him so all, near and far, know of him. Throw back
your heads and sing, sing—sing songs of praise that tell the story of
his wonders. Revel in the name of the Holy One, have merry hearts,
you seekers of God. Keep searching for him and his strong right arm,
strive to live more consciously in his presence in the depth of con-
templation. Keep before your mind's eye all the wonderful things he
has done, the great acts of intervention on our behalf. Heirs of Abraham, children of Jacob, he is God Almighty.

He never forgets a promise, the covenant made to last a thousand
generations, sealed between himself and Abraham, Isaac, and Jacob,
an everlasting bond with Israel. Of Canaan he said, "Take it, it's your
legacy." When they were just a pitiful few, nomads on the earth, ever
on the move from border to border, from nation to nation, God allowed no one to lay a finger on them; not even royalty escaped rebuke on their behalf: "Steer clear of my anointed ones, do you hear?
Not one hair on the head of any of my prophets is to be touched."

He visited famine on the land, cutting off their supply of bread. In
his divine plan, he placed Joseph in a position where he could help
his brothers by allowing him to be sold as a slave. He was chained
like a criminal, shackled like a common thief, until God's moment
came and he put the rest of his plan into action. He softened the heart
of the ruler, so that he released Joseph, gave him complete freedom,
and made him a person of preeminence besides. Now he was made
overseer of all the royal goods, with full authority over all the offi-
cials so that his opinions were sought and valued even by his elders.

The chosen people found their way to Egypt, and God made them prosper and multiply; soon they outnumbered the Egyptians and became a threat to them. Their tolerance turned to fear and hatred, and brutal oppression was the order of the day. God countered by raising up Moses and Aaron as his elected instruments to work his will.

What marvels they performed in his name, what wondrous signs! God plunged the nation into darkness but the Egyptians remained unmoved. Again he acted, bloodying their streams and rivers so that anything living in them died. Then frogs swarmed over the land, not even the royal palace escaped the invasion. Next, God spoke and clouds of flies and gnats billowed into every corner of the country from border to border. Instead of rain, they got pelting hail; raging fires devastated the crops and countryside. Their precious vineyards and fruit trees, all their forests went up in smoke. Again God spoke and the sky was darkened by millions of locusts and grasshoppers, the ground underfoot crackled with them as they devoured everything in sight. Not a blade of grass, not an ear of corn remained. Last of all, Death itself, grim and relentless, stalked the land, taking the firstborn of human and beast alike in one long night of horror.

It was enough. Israel was freed! They poured out of Egypt, loaded down with all the gold and silver they could carry. All of them hale and hearty, untouched by the plagues. Their tormentors had paid them to go, gladly, for their hatred of them had now turned to sickening fear. God covered their march with a protective cloud and at night a mysterious column of fire stood sentinel. When they cried out in hunger, he answered with plentiful quail, and they ate the bread he sent from heaven to their heart's content. At his command, water poured out from the very rocks to quench their thirst, gushed out in abundance, making rivers in the parched waterless land.

He was faithful to what he had promised to his friend Abraham— he led his chosen ones to freedom as they sang and shouted for sheer joy. He gave them their pick of the lands they passed through, dispossessing whole nations, securing them for his people. Everything they found they laid claim to—houses, farms, fortifications, everything theirs for the taking. Yes, everything was theirs forever . . . if they remained loyal and obedient to his laws.

Hallelujah!

106

S HOW YOUR GRATITUDE TO GOD for all his goodness to you; his store of kindness is inexhaustible. Who could ever gauge all the good he has done or ever praise him enough? The obedient are always at peace, and the lot of those on the side of righteousness is happiness.

O God, please don't overlook me when you're passing out blessings. Think of me when it's time to choose those to be saved. Give me a part in the prosperity of your intimates, let me share in their joy and join in their festive celebrations.

We've been bad, all of us, parents and children alike, we've behaved abominably toward you. Our ancestors, while in Egypt, were slow to understand all you had done for them. How easily they forgot the many kindnesses and reprieves you granted; so much so, they actually rose up in rebellion at the Red Sea.

But true to his name, true to himself, he rescued them from their troubles, giving more proof before the whole world of his power to save. His voice rolled over the waters of the Red Sea and they simply fell back and disappeared. God led his people to safety over ground as dry as desert, plucking them right out of the clutches of their pursuers. The enemy met a violent end, swallowed by the sea; no one was spared. Then his people believed in him, shaking the air with their praises.

But all too soon they were back to their old ways and blundered ahead through the desert, not seeking his guidance. They gave in to their lustful impatience and defied him to his face. His yielding to their whining was two-edged because a punishing disease followed hard on its heels. Then the people turned on Moses and Aaron in bitter jealousy and envy, splitting the camp into rival factions. But an earthquake soon put an end to their bickering; it devoured the ringleaders, Dathan, Abiram, and the rest all consumed in the holocaust.

Further imbecilities followed as the people turned to idol-worship, bowing before a golden calf of their own making, heedlessly exchanging God's glory for the effigy of a cud-chewing animal. Everything God had done for them was swept from their minds, Egypt, the Red Sea—everything. It was the last straw. God raised his hand to destroy them all, but Moses, loyal Moses, leapt to their defense, begging and pleading until finally the ultimate punishment was averted. If only the people had reformed . . . but not they.

Now they took to finding fault with Canaan, refusing to believe what God had told them of its beauties and richness. Rebels in the camp fanned their discontent and the people sulked in their tents, refusing to give God any heed. First idol-worship, sacrilegious meals, now this. God finally had his fill; sick of their disloyalty, he promised that not one of them would enter the Promised Land—and their children would be dispersed among strangers.

He acted swiftly, plague suddenly swept the camp, fever, cramps, vomiting, violent death. A universal howl arose until Phineas, an unsung hero, took matters into his own hands, and divining God's wrath, sought out and destroyed those who had instigated the rebellion. As if by magic, the plague ceased and Phineas' place in history was assured.

New provocations arose at Meribah, and this time it was poor Moses who ran afoul of the Lord, because he allowed bitterness and frustration to trap him into rash and thoughtless words. The sins of the people had provoked him beyond endurance, for they had disobeyed God's orders to exterminate the pagans. Instead, they had fawningly fraternized with them, buying their goods, marrying their daughters, picking up their filthy customs, worshiping their idols. Not satisfied with this, they sank to the lowest depths of depravity and offered their very own little ones as sacrifices. Hebrew children sacrificed to pagan gods—the ground soaked up their blood. God's fury raged; he loathed the very sight of them now. The enemy overran them and he didn't lift a finger to help; he just stood there and let them be shackled and enslaved by brutal overlords. Deserved punishment for their ingratitude after all the mercy he had lavished on them.

He hardened his heart but their cries were too much for him, he couldn't blot out the remembrance of the covenant they had made together. In spite of their blatant guilt, he breathed a weary sigh and relented at last. Their lot improved noticeably, to the amazement of their captors, who watched amazed as they thrived in spite of their hardships.

"O dear God," they cried, "please save us. Bring us together again because your people are dispersed in cruel bondage among the nations. We want to praise and thank you once more as one people." Blessed be the God of Israel, who had no beginning and has no end.

Let everyone join in and shout, "Amen!"
Hallelujah!

Book V

Psalms 107–150

THANK THE LORD FOR HIS ENDLESS MERCY; how good he is. All who've had living experience of his love should give thanks, all who've been snatched out of the clutches of persecutors and brought home from exile, from all the corners of the earth. What terrible trials they had—lost and helpless in deserts, dying of hunger and thirst. Close to complete annihilation, they croaked feebly to the Lord for help. God's answer was immediate, they stumbled onto the paths leading to towns and relief. So I say again, let them show their gratitude for all God has done for them out of pure mercy, meeting all the needs of body and soul.

There were some who languished in solitary confinement, chained up in dark, cold misery. They brought this on themselves by their willful disobedience—God let them be overrun by their enemies and suffer the horrors of forced labor, without a shred of pity or a ray of hope. Once again their bleating touched his heart and once again he stepped in. Prison gates flew open, chains fell. Show your gratitude—his mercy is wondrous. Neither iron nor bronze can withstand his onslaught.

Others, broken in mind and body by drink and licentiousness, lay sick as dogs, unable to sleep, unable to eat, begging for death. He released them, too, from their torments, healing their bodies, calming their fears; they should thank him for his mercies and wonders toward us, offer due sacrifices, tell everyone what he's done.

Seafaring folk, those whose whole life is the oceans, have daily proof of God's mighty works—the wonders of the deep, the marvel and variety of his creation. And the storms! How the ocean tosses ships up to the skies and then sends them crashing down again. Everyone loses heart, panic reigns, everyone staggers from bow to stern—the ship's wheel spinning untended, all their knowledge useless, they can do nothing but scream in utter terror, sheer bedlam.

But in all this chaos God is alert to the sound of their cries and his saving hand reaches out to them. At once the winds drop, the sea shudders into stillness, and now it's cries of relief that split the air. A shout, "Land, there's land!" and they know they'll soon ride in safe harbor. God indeed deserves hosannas for the astounding miracles he's worked for his children. A tale to be told wherever people gather, a song of praise to be sung at the city gates.

God can do anything. Marshlands become deserts; flowing wells, dry holes; fertile lands, an arid, salty waste. This is how he punishes sin. And he can do the opposite—bring water and fruitfulness where there was none, providing food and lodging for the poor so that towns and cities spring up like magic. They till the land, plowing, planting, harvesting hand over fist. Families spread and multiply because of his blessing, and their herds share in the universal fertility.

Their evil-eyed pursuers join forces and again subdue them, reducing them and all they own to dust. But not for long. The Lord steps in and all the looted wealth or powerful positions of those vile oppressors can't save them. Like fools they blunder about trying to find a way out of the desert and perish there. But God raises up his people again, giving them twice as much as they had before. How dumbfounded their enemies, how delighted their friends.

The wise will do well to ponder these things and gain wisdom from the lessons of the past, from the Lord's tender mercies toward his own.

I'M READY, LORD, READY. I'll sing, yes, sing your praises with all my soul. Wake up, you stringed instruments, we're going to make the sun rise! I'll go out among the crowds, travel throughout all the nations with my songs of thanksgiving. My song will rise to you from among all the peoples, Lord.

O God, when it comes to goodness and right, the sky's the limit with you. May you be exalted higher than the heavens and your majesty tower over the whole earth; then we can fully expect deliverance—put out your strong arm to save us; hear me, O Lord.

God's voice came to me, "Rejoicing in triumph, I'll divide Shechem and Succoth as I see fit. Gilead, mine, and Manasseh too; Ephraim a strong defense, Judah the seat of my power. But I'll wipe my feet on Moab and stake my claim over Edom. I'll cross over Philistia in victory."

But, Lord, when is all this going to happen? Where's my guide to this strong city? Who'll show me the way to Edom? Have you disowned us, Lord? Aren't you going to accompany us in battle? We need your help God, there's nothing to hope for from human beings. But with you on our side, there's no one who can stand up against us.

O GOD, YOU WHOM I SO PRAISE, why so silent? They've mounted a bitter persecution against me and I'm the target of vicious slander. They've formed a cordon of hatred around me, flinging their lying accusations in my face—a totally unprovoked attack. So this is how they repay my friendship, by treachery—but all I offer is peace. In exchange for goodness I'm ill-used; for my love I get cold hatred.

Well, I can do that too. I can say, "Let them be bowed under a cruel taskmaster, and let them be yoked to an implacable enemy. When they come before the law, let them be found guilty as charged and everything they say be held against them. May they come to an untimely end and all they have pass over into strange hands. Yes, and don't spare their families; let them drink their full measure and be reduced to begging and scraping. Their estates, too, let them be eaten up by their creditors and all their goods carted off. Let them never again hear a kind word, and after they're wiped out, may no one show any pity to their widows and orphans. Away with them altogether—not one left to carry on their names. Only their sins to remain in benighted memory. Yes, and those of all their ancestors too. Don't even spare their mothers. Keep the memory of their iniquities alive so that the whole race of them vanishes.

"Let all these calamities fall on them. They never did a kindness to anyone but terrorized the poor and added to the suffering of the down-and-out. Well, since they were so free with condemnations, may curses be all they ever get. They'd never stoop to wish another well, oh no, not them! Curses were as familiar to them as the clothes on their backs, they were a tonic to them altogether. May they be entangled in a web of miseries themselves, trussed up in a straightjacket of misfortunes."

This is how God will repay my enemies, those who curse and slander me. O Lord God, let's promote your glory together by your loving kindness toward me. I'm the most miserable of human beings; they've broken my heart by the sheer malice of their accusations. My time is running out and fasting has sapped the last bit of my strength. Ridicule is all I inspire, people look at me and turn away with a snort of disgust. Help me, Lord, be merciful, and all will see that you're on my side.

Your blessings will deflect their curses; shame-faced they'll beat a hasty retreat and I'll roar with delight. Give it to them, Lord! Pile disgrace upon disgrace on them, roll them in it; then heartfelt thanks will burst from my lips, then I'll shout out the news far and wide, telling everyone that God stands by his friends to save them from unjust condemnation.

A MESSAGE FROM GOD TO MY LORD: "Sit here on my right, in the place of honor, while I reduce your enemies to dirt under your feet." Yes, your authority stems from God's seat of power, Zion itself. Your enemies are in your power; dominate them. The people will willingly follow your lead, for your majesty is radiant as the dawn and your youth eternally fresh and dewy.

God will not go back on his sworn word: "I anoint you a priest forever, in a direct line from Melchizedek." With him at your side not even rulers will escape his wrath. Body will be piled on body and heads will roll in every direction. Because he can refresh himself at wayside streams in peace, he will be able to hold his head high, his conquest complete.

Hallelujah!
I'll thank the Lord with all my heart in plain sight of the holy council and public alike. What marvelous things he does, ingenious, delightful. Eagerly prayed for by the needy. This act glorious, that one majestic. Endless wonders. His works are a monument to his kindness and compassion.

He never forgets his commitment to feed the faithful. He's displayed his great powers before the dazzled eyes of his people, despoiling whole nations to enrich and establish his own. His right hand is justice, his left hand steadfastness, his word certainty. Solidly based on absolute truth, his works are indestructible. Having saved his people from disaster time and again, he asks only that they be obedient to his commandments forever. Oh, how awesome and holy is our God!

Those who revere the Lord are well on the road to wisdom; the gaining of deep insight into God's mysteries is their reward. His praises are everlasting.

HALLELUJAH!
They're the happy ones, those who know and revere God, doing his will with joyful zest. Their offspring will be influential in high places and pass on their good standing to the generations after them. Everything they touch will turn to gold and nothing can ever tarnish their good name. God will be a shining beacon for them, lighting their way out of every difficulty, and they will be kind, compassionate, and just.

Ever ready to lend a hand to their needier neighbors and scrupulously correct in all their dealings, they themselves can count on unending good fortune and their place in history is assured. Troubles will never shake their faith in God, and supported by complete reliance on their Lord, they fear nothing even though surrounded by foes. They have lavishly given to help others, they will lavishly receive praise and honors.

Their enemies will fume, eaten up by rage and envy, doomed to utter frustration.

psalm 113

HALLELUJAH!
Praise the Lord! Come on, let's hear it—Praise the Lord!
Blessed be the name of the Lord, forever and ever. Let his praises ring
from horizon to horizon. How high he is above us, higher than the
heavens themselves. Who or what can compare with the majesty of
him seated on his glorious throne above? Yet not too high to take note
of puny us—he rescues the poor from their wretchedness, responds
to the cries of the despairing, giving them new dignity so they can
hold up their heads again, even walk among the great and mighty.

He blesses the childless wife with children and sets her over a
happy, bustling household.

Oh yes! Hallelujah!

WHEN ISRAEL WAS LIBERATED FROM EGYPT, rescued from those strange-sounding people, God set Judah aside as his special abode and put his mark on Israel. The sea took one look and shrank back in terror, yes, the waters of the Jordan turned and raced away in a panic. The mountains shook themselves, bounded like giant rams and the foothills took to kicking up their heels like frisky yearlings.

Tell us, seas, what made you run? You, Jordan, why the panic? And all these cavortings, you mountains and hills, what do they mean? You do well to shake in your boots, earth, for you are in the presence of the all-holy God of Jacob, the One who can form pools of water in rock beds and cause bubbling springs to burst from flint.

psalm 115

ALMIGHTY GOD, WE'RE NOT WORTHY OF PRAISE. It's you who's done it all, you who are so loving and true. Why do these people keep on asking, "And just where is this God of theirs?" In heaven, that's where. And whatever he wills, he does. But these idols they worship—nothing, little tin gods dipped in gold or silver, pieces of junk turned out by the dozen. Mouths that can't utter a word, eyes that can't see anything. No sound can penetrate those ears, and their noses can't smell a thing. What can their hands feel, and where can their feet take them? Not one sound will ever come from their hollow throats. The ones who make these things are as empty-headed as their handiwork, and those who pray to them are worse.

Israel, trust in God; he is our helper and protector. And you descendants of Aaron, trust in God; he is our helper and protector. All of you who revere God, trust him; he is our helper and protector.

The Lord has not forgotten us; no, he blesses us and he will bless the people of Israel and the descendants of Aaron. Yes, everyone who honors him will be blessed, from the highest to the lowest.

Friends, God blesses you and grants you prosperity, you and all who come after you. You chosen ones are blessed by the Lord, Creator of heaven and earth; heaven is his domain, but the green earth belongs to humankind. Remember, the dead can no longer sing God's praises, all those who have passed into oblivion. But we, the living, can send up our praises unendingly and forever.

Hallelujah!

psalm 116

HOW GOOD GOD IS to answer my prayers. I love him so! Confident of his ever ready help, I know I can count on him for anything I might need for the rest of my life. So listen.

I was at the point of death, searing pain, a red haze around me, hemming me in; my heart broken by grief and helplessness. Sobbing weakly, I managed to pray, "O God, God, I beg you, have mercy." I tell you, there's no one like him, no kindness or compassion like his. No one is too insignificant, too low to be noticed—he especially loves the little ones. I was in need and he had to help. Be at peace my soul, we're in God's hands.

My God, you've granted me a reprieve, dried my eyes, and removed all obstacles from my path. I can hold up my head again, I throb with life again! [Ps. 115] I tell you people, honestly, I was really in desperate straits; I had no faith left in anyone. "Liars!" I shouted, "You're all lying to me. I'm dying!"

What can I do now for God who's done so much for me? How can I show my gratitude? I know—the temple. I'll give witness to my gratitude there in front of them all, making thank-offerings and fulfilling the vows I made during my ordeal. Surely, the death of one of his servants costs dearly.

O Lord, I'm all yours now, your slave, as my mother was before me. You've freed me from the threat of death. My thanksgiving sacrifices and praises will mingle in one hymn of adoration of the Lord's name. Every vow will be paid to the letter in front of witnesses, there in the courts of God's house, set like a jewel in the heart of Jerusalem.

Hallelujah!

COME ON, YOU NATIONS OF THE WORLD, join us in praising the Lord. Yes, everyone, everywhere. His merciful love and his truth are infinite.

Hallelujah!

psalm

118

O GIVE THANKS TO GOD FOR HIS GOODNESS, his mercy is infinite. Israel, acknowledge that his mercy is infinite. Descendants of Aaron, you too must say, "His mercy is infinite."

Everyone who reveres the Lord shout, "His mercy is infinite!"

Listen to me. In the midst of terrible distress I had only to cry out to him and his answer boomed out from heaven. With God on my side nothing can touch me. Threats? I laugh them off. I tell you, God is fighting for me in the midst of my foes, and I'll have the satisfaction of seeing my enemies wiped out.

How much better it is to trust in God than in puny mortals; how much safer one is in his company than in the houses of the rich and powerful. I'm surrounded by enemy nations but in God's name I'll cut my way through them. They bay at me, swarm all over me, but in God's name I'll slash through them. Their fierce attack envelops me like a cloud of hornets, but I'll quickly drive them back and with God's help wipe them out.

You evil fiends, you thought you had me, didn't you. You didn't count on the Lord—the strength in my arms, the song in my heart, the very life of me. Do you hear the sounds of victory pouring from the temple? God's done this, God himself. God's triumphed again by the strength of his mighty arm. So I'm not doomed to death; I'm to live on to become a witness to God's transforming love. He tried me, sorely, but not to the point of extinction. So fling wide the temple gates, let me in—I've a song of thanksgiving to sing. Through these blessed gates pours the happy worshiping throng. Thank you Lord. Thank you for listening to me.

Look, everyone. Israel, the stone tossed aside as worthless, now shines as the cornerstone of everything. God's done this—what a wonderful sight. This day was made in heaven, let's enjoy and revel in every minute of it. Dear God, love us always, champion us always, let everything we do succeed. Happy the pilgrim who comes in God's name, greeted with shouted blessings from the temple steps. God is a mighty God, the very light of our eyes. Cut branches of palm and olive and come in procession, form living garlands of tribute in his honor. I'm all yours my God, I'll praise and thank you with all my strength. Be grateful, friends, to our God, our good God; his mercy is endless.

119

HOW REWARDING IT IS TO EXERCISE undivided allegiance to God, absolute fidelity to his laws. What joys for those who make his divine commandments their lives, who give their whole being to the search for God. How studiously they avoid evil, willingly choosing the straight way. You wish it, Lord, giving us a code to live by and commandments to observe it. Would that my behavior was governed by it. Then I wouldn't flush with shame when faced with your statutes. How grateful I'll be once I've turned fully to you and the observance of the law. I'll be faithful, Lord, don't abandon me.

I ask myself: How can the young stay clean, how rule their conduct according to your will, Lord? I've poured my whole soul into the search for you; help me, protect me from myself. I hug your commandments to my heart, plunging them into the deeps of my being, lest I blunder into sin. All-holy God, show me how best to serve you. I can recite every law from memory now, glorying in the richness of it all, even more than in stores of gold and silver. Your commandments are the food of my meditations as delight fills my soul. I'll never forget them, I promise!

Be good to me Lord, give me life and strength and I'll keep your commandments. Open my eyes to see the wonders that come from devout observance. I long for heaven; this earth is foreign to me. Show me yourself through the law. I'm obsessed by my desire to always be a true believer and doer of your will. How you rebuke the arrogant, those who bring a curse on themselves by their wanton disobedience. Don't let me fall into that trap and come under that sentence; I've tried to serve you truly. I turn my back on the gossip and plots hatched against me by those in power; you're my sole concern. I've only one joy, the Lord; I've only one delight, keeping the law.

I'm crushed under a weight of troubles and grief; pour fresh life into me as you've promised. I've openly revealed my sinful past and you've forgiven me; now teach me the right way to live. Make your laws clear for me so that I can fruitfully meditate on them. I'm soul-sick with remorse; give me strength—you promised. Heal me of the habit of lying; teach me, I'm anxious to learn. I've made my choice—your way, your law, this is my one objective. Don't shame me in front of my detractors by not supporting me. With your help what progress I'll make, how my heart will expand to embrace the universe.

Teach me your laws, O Lord, and I'll obey to the end of my days. Enlighten me and I'll be faithful and observe the commandments with all my heart. Point out the right paths; I already know the joys of obedience. Give me a taste for the things that are true and lasting so I can turn my back on empty glitter. Help me to resist temptation by granting me a clean outlook on life. Stand by your promises to the one who serves you. Shield me from the ridicule I dread; I know I'm right in following you. You know my longing for spiritual growth; admit me to intimate friendship.

Cover me with your mercies, O Savior, according to your promises. Armed this way, I can face down my taunters with one word, relying on your inspiration. May this inspiration never be far from me, it's my one hope. I'll never go back on the law, never, never, never. Nothing can make me stumble since I seek the right thing, nothing; and I wouldn't fear to speak out in the face of the powerful of the earth, without a blush. Your commandments are my soul's delight, how I love them. With upraised hands I'll chant a litany of love in honor of them, making my meditation on them alone.

Your promises have inspired me with hope; never forget them, please. The recollection of them sustains me in all my suffering and puts new life into me. The proud and arrogant have mocked me to my face; their persecution stems from my strict adherence to your law, but I'm undaunted in my observance of it. I draw strength from my remembrance of how you deal with the proud and am consoled in my trials even as I burn with indignation at their brazen disobedience. To me your decrees are like music, hymns to be sung in worship. The thought of them never leaves me, following me even into my dreams, so that I'm inspired to ever greater acts of fidelity.

I've publicly proclaimed that my vocation is to follow you, Lord, and to live by your laws. Please answer the prayers I say to you with all my heart. After seeing what a life I was leading, I was converted and seized with the yearning to give up everything to follow you. They try to force me to revert to my old ways but I'm adamant. In the night I rise to pray and to thank you for enlightening me. Your friends are my friends now. How good you are. Tell me what you want me to do and I'll do it.

O Lord, not one promise you've made has gone unfulfilled. Teach me how to use my head; I'm completely in your hands. I was unmanageable, I know it, until troubles came—now, all I want is to be led. How good you are, how much good you do; show me what I should do in order to be like you. No matter how many slanderous rumors are spread about me, I stand firm. How callous they are, how hard of heart, incapable of compassionate feeling. But I, thanks to your saving help, delight in keeping your law; why, all the gold and silver in the world is nothing in comparison.

O God, I'm a creature of your making; give me insight so I can serve you with intelligence. I want all your friends to rejoice in my good fortune, the result of my unwavering trust. Everything you do is right, even the suffering you allow to come my way. Send me only a word of consolation, temper your justice with mercy so I have the courage to go on. Oh, how I love your law; may my lying enemies get what they richly deserve, but may I be granted deeper and deeper insight into your mysteries. Let me be an example of steadfastness for all who serve you and let me be honest and true in your service so that I don't ever die of shame!

I'm burning up with longing for you, breathless with hope. My eyes are streaming for some sign of relief; I moan, "When? Where are you?" I'm consumed, shriveled with this yearning, I think of you unceasingly. How long must I wait, how long before you punish my tormentors? Look at the vicious traps laid for me by the completely unscrupulous. I follow a just God, a faithful God; their persecution is senseless. Help me. A little more and they would've made an end of me had it hadn't been for my fidelity. Come to me with life and mercy and I'll continue in unabated fidelity to your commandments.

Your law is divine, unchangeable, unending. Your fidelity spans the ages and the world you created stands firm, just as it came from your hands. All creation obeys you, everything serves you. If you hadn't given me joy in your service, I never would've had the courage to go on. I'll never forget you; your laws are life, I belong to you. Then help me; I've tried so hard to be faithful. Although the villainous are plotting against me, they can't drive your commandments from my heart. How limited and ephemeral is human perfection, but yours, Lord, is endless, holding all possibilities.

Lord, I'm in love with your law, I can think of nothing else; what power this gives me over my enemies. How much more insight I have than those who are supposed to teach me, for I ruminate endlessly on your precepts. I seem to know more than my elders because my obedience is equal to, even surpasses their years of experience. How careful

I am that not the least inadvertent slip should tarnish my observance. I feel that you yourself have become my instructor, so pure is my grasp of the law. I roll the words on my tongue like sweet tidbits, like morsels of the sweetest honeycomb. So clear is my perception of the difference between right and wrong, I have all the strength I need to resist temptation.

Your words are like lamps lighting up the path in front of me. I've sworn and now reaffirm my intention to never forsake the law. But I'm sick, Lord; please help me. Please accept my praise and tell me why this is happening to me. I risk my life time and again in serving you and never turn back. They try to stop me but I go on. Your law is a precious legacy, a treasure I exult in; I'm prepared to serve you with all my heart to the end.

The lukewarm are an abhorrence to me; I burn with love for your law. You're everything to me—protection, refuge. I've put my entire hope in your promises. You sinners, keep your distance; don't try to force your way between me and my God. Stand behind me, Lord, support my claim so I don't suffer the shame of disappointment. Be my defense and I'll have the strength to continue in fidelity. I know what happens to your foes: you grind them into the dust; their lying mouths can't help them there. All who are faithless suffer the same fate, swept aside like the worthless trash they are; that's why I love you so much. The sight of their punishment makes me tremble, and I shiver at the awesome responsibility of keeping the law.

I've done my best to do right; don't let me fall into the hands of my enemies. Support my efforts; don't let them crush me. I wait and wait for a sign of rescue, for a sound that will tell me you're on your way. Mercy, Lord, guide me, Lord. Since I belong to you, give me some insight that will help me to serve you as I should. It's time for action, Lord; the law is being desecrated, the law, the blessed law I love more than finest gold. Every last word is precious, while I don't give *that* for anything these hypocrites have to offer.

I keep your laws with all my soul because they're truly wonderful. When you flood the intellect with light, even a simpleton can understand. I'm famished, panting to know your commands; look at me, admit me into your intimate friendship as you've done for others. Confirm me in love and free me from the tyranny of the senses; keep oppressors far away from me so I can serve you freely. Bless me, take me under your wing and teach me. When I see how your laws are ignored, I collapse in tears.

How just and fair you are, O God, how reliable your word. Everything you've put into your code is balanced, sane, and absolutely right. The sight of my hard-hearted enemies fans the passion of my zeal for your law; it consumes me. Your least word is priceless, I'm in love with it. I may be insignificant, a nobody, but I've one boast—my loyalty to the law. Your justice is everlasting because you're everlasting and there's not a false note in the entire law. Troubles have been coming down on me, and your commands are my only consolation; like you, they're an unending delight. Enlighten me and I'll make full use of them.

Oh, how I've cried, Lord, answer, please; I promise you I'll obey. Listen to my sobbing; save me, and I'll dedicate the rest of my days to your service. I'm up way before dawn, praying, entreating you, relying on your promises. All night long I meditate on your precepts— no sleep for me. Won't you listen, won't you answer? Have mercy. Forgive me so I can take heart. My enemies stalk me, Lord, waiting for their chance. What do they know about your law? But I feel you near me and I know that your commandments are unchanging. I've always known this, that your decrees are eternal.

Lord, look at the state I'm in, pity me; I haven't been false to you, I swear it. Take up my cause and obtain my acquittal, infuse new life into me in keeping with the covenant between us. The wicked—lost, the whole pack of them, scorners of the law. O God, how sweet is your mercy; let me experience it once again. I may be hounded by the enemy, but nothing and no one can make me deviate from the path of obedience. I'm sickened by the treachery of those infidels who don't give *that* for your law. But see how devout I am, O Lord, and repay me accordingly. Every word of the law is tried and true and meant to endure forever.

The powerful of this world persecute me senselessly, but I'm in awe only of your word; how happy it makes me, like finding buried treasure. I abhor and detest lies but adore your law. Seven times a day I faithfully recite my litanies of praise because it's only right. What a cause for peace this is to the faithful, what a help to them in their tribulations. Dear God, I've firmly hoped for my ultimate salvation, unswervingly obedient to your decrees. I love and obey the law with all my soul, following every commandment to the letter, confident that you know me through and through.

Lord, hear my cries of anguish and cast your light into the darkness of my soul, as you've promised. Listen to my pleading—as you've promised. How I'll praise you once you've taught me how. I'll respond fully to all you ask, for you ask only what is right and good. But help me—I'm committed to you. Oh, how I yearn for you, my Salvation, how I revel in the law. Give me life and breath to praise you, strengthen me through your commandments. I've wandered away like a stray sheep; seek me out because your law is written on my heart.

I PRAYED THAT GOD WOULD SAVE ME—"O Lord, deliver me from liars and hypocrites!"—and he did. So, prepare yourself, villain. Have you any idea of the fate that awaits you, of what is about to happen to you, you two-faced traitor? Expert sharpshooters will riddle you with arrows, burning coals will rain down on you.

But my fate is worse than being doomed to wander among the pagans of Meshech, to be a tent-dweller in Kedar. And why? I'm a peaceable person forced to live among those who hate me. My words of peace trigger only war, war, war.

psalm
121

I STRAIN MY EYES, LOOKING, searching the hills for a sign of rescue. Where will my help come from? The help I need can only come from God, Maker of heaven and earth.

Don't be afraid. He takes care of you, keeps you from stumbling. The One watching over you isn't asleep or drowsy; rest easy, Israel's Savior is ever alert and watchful. This is the truth; God guards you, hovers over you protectingly. No need to fear the searing noonday heat or the mysterious influence of the moon.

Trust him. God will shield you from all dangers to body or soul. He'll be by your side in all your coming and going, to the very last.

psalm 122

HOW EAGERLY I ACCEPTED THEIR INVITATION, "Come on, come with us up to the Lord's house." Oh, the joy of it, to stand at last within your gates, O Jerusalem. Look at it, look at this beautiful city; what symmetry, what unity. All the people of Israel converge on it, united in one common goal, rendering jubilant thanks to God. From of old Jerusalem was chosen to be judge over us, everything decided there, the royal seat always there.

Peace, let's pray for the peace of Jerusalem. Yes, my beloved, those who love you are well rewarded. Peace in your streets, may peace and prosperity radiate from your very towers. In the name of all my relatives and friends I wish you unending peace. All this because the holy place is in your midst.

G OD IN HEAVEN, I'll keep my eyes raised to you in prayer and entreaty. I'm like a slave searching his master's face for a sign; no servant girl could be more riveted on her mistress's slightest wish than we are on our Lord until he responds.

Mercy, Lord, mercy; we are sick to death of the mockery and contempt of our pot-bellied, arrogant oppressors.

I F GOD HADN'T BEEN ON OUR SIDE—Israel can really say this—hadn't
been with us through it all when they came against us in all their
fury, we would've been wiped off the face of the earth. We would've
been plunged down into the depths, drowned like rats. Annihilated.

But thanks be to God, he didn't let it happen. We're free—free;
the trap was sprung and off we went, free as birds. All we have to do
is call on him by name, the Creator of heaven and earth, and help
comes at once.

THOSE WHO TRUST IN GOD are as unshakable as Mount Zion itself, that everlasting mountain. Just as Jerusalem is encircled by mountains, so God's people enjoy his encircling protection, always. No evil leanings can ever take root among us, lest the good but weak be tempted and perish.

O God, be the reward of the faithful and steadfast, but deal ruthlessly with defectors so that having thrown their lot in with the enemy they may all perish together.

Let Israel enjoy true peace, within and without.

WHEN GOD RELEASED ZION FROM CAPTIVITY, we thought we were dreaming. We laughed like loons, sang like songbirds, we were so happy. We were the talk of the nations. "Look!" they gasped. "Look, their God has great plans for these people!" Well, God has done wonders for us, we're delirious with joy.

Now, Lord, help us put our lives back together again; help us reap a great harvest from the soil we've soaked with our tears. Surely those who've sown in bitterness and sorrow will come home, arms full of fragrant sheaves, shouting out the good news.

I F GOD'S NOT PART OF THE PLAN, no use trying to build. If God doesn't protect the sleeping city, what good is a watchman? It's useless for you to rise early and work late into the night to gain a livelihood. Don't you realize God's favorites don't have any worries? God rewards the right living with a fine big family. Having sons while still young is like being well armed—the more sons, the more secure the family, and they can be proud of their father when together they face down his enemies.

BLESSED ARE THE GOD-FEARING AND OBEDIENT. You'll sit down at a well-laden table, secure and happy in the knowledge that your hard work has earned it all for you. Your dear wife will be strong and healthy. And the children—a circle of shining faces around your table, growing up sturdy and tall as olive trees. Feast your eyes. This is the Lord's reward to the honest. God will shower blessing on you from Mount Zion and never let you be exiled from Jerusalem, ever. Yes, and you'll have the joy of bouncing many grandchildren on your knee.

God's blessings on Israel!

O H, THE TROUBLES I'VE HAD ALL MY LIFE, says Israel, troubles, troubles one after another, yet I'm still on my feet. My back is crisscrossed with scars from repeated whipping, long deep furrows. But God is good, he's broken their power over me. May they suffer utter disgrace and ruination, these haters of Zion. Let them be like scrub grass on the rooftops, utterly worthless, never enough to fill your fist, let alone bind into sheaves. No passerby would even think to honor it with a blessing.

psalm 130

FROM THE DEPTHS OF MY MISERY I cry out to you, my God. Please listen to me, please attend to my broken words. My God, who can defend themselves if you choose to accuse them? But you have the power to forgive, this power that inspires awe.

I wait and wait, my soul throbs with expectation. I'm like a watcher scanning the horizon for the first light of dawn; no, more intent, more eager. Israel, persevere in this ardent trust, for God is all merciful and all-redeeming. He will save Israel from its sins.

MY GOD, I'M NOT PROUD, not fiercely ambitious, not led about by delusions of grandeur. No, I've finally been gentled, quieted the stormy passions of my soul. Now I'm like a child who's weaned and content to lie quietly on mother's breast, wanting only that. Yes, that's what my soul's like now.

O Israel, share my joy. Let's put our hope in God, forever and ever.

O LORD, BE MINDFUL OF DAVID and all he had to suffer, be mindful of the vows he made to the mighty God of Jacob, "There'll be no sleep for me, I won't even go into my house or allow myself the smallest flicker of an eyelash until I build a place of worship worthy of my God."

The news about the ark had reached Ephrathah, diligent searching led us to it in the countryside around Jaar. Down on your knees! Worship him!

All is in readiness, Lord. Come, Lord, enter this place of rest prepared for you and the ark of your power. Clothe your priests with holiness, fill your people with jubilation. Open your ears to the pleas of your anointed, for David's sake.

This is what God swore to David—and his word is unchangeable—"One of your sons will reign as king. If they're true to me and my law, the royal line will stretch unbroken down through the ages."

God himself has set his heart on Zion, established himself in its midst. "I swear it," says the Lord, "Zion is my own, my darling forever. I'll feed her, satisfy the hunger of her poor. Her priests will be holy, her saints loud in their praises. David's oil will flow unceasingly, his light will never fail. His enemies will be utterly disgraced, but for him a brilliant crown."

psalm
133

A UNITED AND LOVING FAMILY is a beauty to behold. Unity is like fragrant oil poured out, running down in abundance over the head, over the face, yes, even into a beard like Aaron's, soaking the collar of his robes. It's like clouds of mist rolling down the slopes of Mount Hermon, watering the earth. It's there that God gives his greatest blessing, eternal life!

PEACE, YOU MINISTERS OF GOD. Bless him. Bless him, you who keep the all-night vigil. Stand with outstretched hands in the sanctuary, joyfully chanting his praises.

And may God bless you, pilgrims, from the heart of Zion, God the Creator of heaven and earth.

HALLELUJAH!
Praise him, I say; praise his holy name, you ministers, privileged to serve in the inner courts of our God. Shout hallelujahs because he's good, praise his holy name because it's a delight. God's chosen Israel for his own, set Jacob apart as his special treasure—the wonder of it. I know beyond doubt that God's great. What earthly God could compare with him? Whatever he wills is done, everywhere, in the heavens or on the earth, on the oceans or in their deeps. At his word clouds of sea mist rise to the heavens and come back as torrential rains, with the thunderclaps, lightning bolts, and howling winds God unleashes from his store of marvels.

This is the God who annihilated the firstborn of human and beast in Egypt. Listen, Egyptians. He made his awesome presence felt among you by signs and dreadful wonders, spared no one, from Pharaoh himself to the least in his kingdom. Nations collapsed beneath God's charge, mighty rulers simply disappeared, rulers like Sihon of the Amorites, Og of Bashan; and all the Canaanite potentates were reduced to less than nothing. Israel fell heir to their vast holdings, God saw to that; and all their descendants profited by the rout.

How invincible your name, O Lord, burned into the minds and hearts of your people forever. God alone decides the fate of his people, his is the power to grant pardon. As for pagan idols, pah!—mere silver and gold fashioned by human hands. They mold mouths that are dumb, eyes that are sightless, ears that are deaf. Not a single breath will ever pass those lifeless lips. These artisans are as senseless as their handiwork, so is anyone fool enough to pray to them.

But you, Israel, praise the Lord; bless and exalt him, descendants of Aaron. Revere him you devout ones; Levites shout praise. Let Zion resound with his blessings, the praises of Jerusalem's God.
Hallelujah!

HALLELUJAH!
Thank God for all his goodness,
    his love is unending.
Give thanks to the God above all gods,
    his love is never-ending.
Give thanks to the Lord of all lords,
    his love is everlasting.
This God works great wonders unaided,
    yes, his love is unending;
out of the depths of his wisdom, created the heavens,
    for his love is never-ending,
brought land up out of the churning waters,
    his love is unending.
One word and there was light,
    his love is never-ending;
he created the majestic sun, master of day,
    for his love never ends.
and the moon and the stars who hold sway at night,
    his love is without end.
He's the One who brought Egypt to its knees,
    yes, his love is eternal,
freed Israel from bitter bondage,
    for his love is without end,
by his strong right hand and powerful arm,
    for his love is unending.
He divided the Red Sea in two,
    his love is never-ending,
created a safe escape for Israel,
    his love never ends,

but engulfed Pharaoh and all his forces in the Red Sea,
    for his love is without end.
Our God shepherded his people through desert wastes,
    yes, his love never ends,
  Striking down all who dared oppose them, even great and
      magnificent rulers,
    for his love can never end.
Down went Sihon, ruler of the Amorites,
    for his love is unending,
And down went Og, ruler of Bashan,
    truly, his love can never end.
All they owned was given to Israel,
    for his love is never-ending,
Theirs to keep forever and ever,
    his love never ends.
He took pity on our miserable condition,
    for his love can never end,
Fighting our battles, delivering us from the foe,
    truly, his love is unending;
And none, human or beast, need ever go hungry,
    his great love has no end.
Thank him, thank him unceasingly,
    for the love of the God of heaven indeed has no end.

psalm
137

S ITTING BY THE RIVERS OF BABYLON, sunk in misery, we couldn't
hold back the tears. We wept bitterly, recalling our beloved Zion.
Our guitars hung, silent and still, from willow branches; no music
for us. Our captors, tormentors, mocked us. "Come on," they jeered,
"let's hear some songs from the old country. Cheer up! Give us a
tune, huh?" How could they ask us to make merry in that place, so
far from home.

O my Jerusalem, I would as soon have my right arm paralyzed as
forget you for one instant. Sing? I'd sooner never speak again than
let you fade from my thoughts, never take pleasure in anything else.
Dear God, never forget what the Edomites did to Jerusalem. My ears
still ring with their bestial cries of "Tear it down, down, level it to
the ground!"

Your time will come, spawn of Babylon, destroyer. Blessed are
those who are going to avenge us, who'll do to you as you've done to
us. They'll have the inexpressible joy of trampling every one of you
under their heels.

psalm
138

I'LL THANK YOU, GOD, thank you with all my heart. My song of praise will put even the angels to shame. Prostrate in the dust before your holy temple, my cries of gratitude for your great mercy, for your very Being, will ring in the ears of all who behold me. You've gone far, far beyond my greatest expectations, outdone even Yourself. Your answer to my pleading has me bursting with exultation, my soul can hardly bear it.

Rulers who hear of you will join in thanksgiving; they too will sing loudly, praising the ways of the Lord because the glorious Lord is great. He may be in heaven on high, but he watches over the lowly and scrutinizes the ways of the proud and the arrogant.

Whenever troubles come down on me, you give me hope. Soon my enemies are in flight and I'm rescued. God has begun a great work in me and will see it to its perfect accomplishment. O God, your mercy is endless; you'll never abandon any of your creatures.

O LORD, YOU SEE RIGHT THROUGH ME, you know me like a book. You watch my every move, you know my every thought. You know if I'm awake or asleep, where all my haunts are. Not a word leaves my lips that catches you unaware. I feel you all around me, wherever I turn, I lie in the palm of your hand.

I can't understand it, my mind's unable to grasp the concept, it's completely beyond me. Where could I go to escape the reach of your Spirit? Where could I turn and not see your reflection? If I soar heavenward, I find you. If I plunge into the deeps, I find you. If I imitated the dawn and dusk that dwell at the far ends of the sea, even there you'd find me out and close your strong hand around me.

If I said, "Surely I can hide under cover of darkness," what night would be black enough to resist your penetrating glance? Dark night is blazing day to you, one is as bright as the other. After all, you made the core of my being, put me together in my mother's womb, fashioning every part of me.

What a marvelous thing is this body of mine, thank you; but everything you do is wonderful. Who could dispute it? Not a bone of my body is a mystery to you; you watched as I was being made in complete darkness. When I was but a speck of matter, you knew me, all the members of my body, all their days, carefully noted in the book of life.

I adore the working of your mind, O Lord—how vast your thought. If I were fool enough to try to trace the pattern, it would be like trying to count grains of sand, counting until I fall asleep from exhaustion, and when I wake finding I've hardly even begun.

Wipe out sinners, Lord; get away from me, you murderers! Which of them dares slander you? Such conceit, such insolence. O God, you can see how much I hate those who hate you, how revolting they are to me. I loathe and detest them with all my soul; they're my enemies now as well as yours. Scrutinize my every thought, O God, probe my innermost heart, see if there's the slightest trace of sin there. Then, Lord, then lead me to eternal life.

140

S AVE ME FROM THE VIOLENT, LORD, protect me from the blood-thirsty who delight in concocting wicked schemes, stirring up war and trouble wherever they go. They're experts in using words like the fangs of a snake, venom fills their mouths. I'm terrified; protect me from them Lord, keep them away. Stand between me and those vile enemies who are hounding my steps, who love to use force to get what they want. What traps they've set for me, as if I were a beast or a bird of prey.

I cried out to God, "You're the Lord of my life, listen to me, O God, O Strong One; more than once you've protected me in the thick of battle. Don't let them catch me, don't let this wicked plot against me succeed, or evil will have triumphed over good. May all the miseries planned for me come down on them, double. Burn them up, send them to hell never to return. Don't let liars rule over us; let them fall by the same violence they visited on others, blow upon blow.

This I believe, that God is always on the side of the downtrodden, always the hope of the poor. The good will give thanks to you and bless your name, O Lord, and live in your presence.

B E QUICK TO HEAR ME, LORD, when I call out to you, be attentive to the sound of my voice. Let my prayer rise up to you like clouds of incense, my upturned palms like an evening sacrifice. O God, teach me how to guard my tongue, post a strong watch at my lips. Help me resist temptation, the lure of a life of crime and easy money, never let me touch one dishonest penny.

I can bear the corrections of the good, they're a blessing; the rebukes of the upright soothe the rebellious soul—never let me be so foolish as to resent them, but let me be unrelenting toward the blandishments of the wicked. Everyday I meet their hatred with prayers, and when those who condemn unjustly are broken into pieces, everyone will know I spoke the truth. The entrance to hell is littered with bones, as though plowed up and torn from the earth. That's all they can expect.

But I never take my eyes from you, O Lord my God; let me take refuge in you, don't let me die. Show me how to avoid their cleverly laid traps, how to thwart their evil plans. Better yet, while I escape, let them blunder into their own traps and be caught like rats.

WITH SHOUTS OF ANGUISH I CRY OUT TO GOD; I plead, entreat, fill the air with a continual din, pouring out all the bitterness of my soul. But even though my courage fails, you're always there, watching every step I take.

Oh, the traps laid out for me. I look to right and left for one friendly face, but all I find are averted eyes; no one wants to know me, no one cares whether I live or die. You're all I have Lord, that's why I cried out, "Lord, my only Hope, my Refuge, all I have in this life!" Rescue me because I'm relentlessly pursued; they're too many for me. Free me so I've got a reason to thank you, to bless your name. I'll gather crowds wherever I go, eager to hear the story of my resurrection.

HEAR ME, O GOD, listen to what I'm saying, pleading for. You're true, you're just; so give me a hearing, don't put me on trial because who can withstand your scrutiny, no one alive is sinless. The enemy hounds me, draining me of all hope; everything's dark, a living death. I've lost the will to live, lost all heart. Memories of past glories rise up to torment me, the things you did for me. How good it was between us then. What went wrong? I raise my trembling hands to you in anguish and despair, my soul dry and cracked open with longing.

Oh please come back to me, I'm dying. If you keep your back stonily turned against me, I might as well be dead. Let this bitter night end in a dawn bright with promise. I know you can do it, I still trust in you. Show me the way out of these troubles; I plead with you. Save me, hide me from my foes.

Teach me obedience, you, my God and Father of my life. Your guidance is best; lead on, show me the way to the land of the just. O God, because of your name, give me life, draw me out of this pit of distress. Come between me and my tormentors, make a swift end of them, all those who want to destroy my very soul. I speak as your humble servant, Lord.

B LESSED BE GOD who gives me strength for the battle. He's every-thing to me, mercy, strength, refuge, rescuer, protector. I turn to him in every need, and he subdues the rebellious under me. O God, what are we to you, what are we, any of us, that you should even spare us a thought? Humankind? It's nothing, its whole existence has no more substance than a fleeting shadow. But you . . . Come, O God, step down from the heavens and come, set the mountains smoldering by your mere touch. Spray the enemy with lightning bolts and fiery arrows until they scatter in headlong flight. Snatch me from the raging waters, from the grasp of these foreign dogs, perjurers who're ever ready to point the finger.

I'll sing anew, Lord, songs of praise on my twelve-string guitar. For you are the One who champions the cause of our rulers, who flies to David's rescue, saves him from his attackers. Yes, save me from foreign dogs, perjurers, and false accusers so that our sons may grow up tall and straight as saplings and our daughters as beautiful as the finest carved temple columns. So that our barns may bulge with every conceivable kind of grain and our flocks multiply by the thousand and ten thousand. So that we always have well-laden carts to pull through a countryside full of peace and prosperity, free from the sound of weeping.

What a heaven on earth for those who bask in such favor, what a joy to be called God's chosen ones!

145

I'LL BOAST LOUDLY OF YOUR GREATNESS, O God, my Lord, forever and ever. Every day a fresh outburst of praise, on and on forever. How great and glorious is God, how worthy of all praise, his glory utterly beyond human comprehension. All ages will praise you, passing on the story of your wonderful deeds to succeeding generations.

You'll be the object of my meditations as I muse lovingly on your glory and honor, and on all the marvels you've performed. Everything will testify to your greatness, as I sing your praises. Your acts will evoke the remembrance of past kindnesses and provide fresh impetus to praise you.

God Almighty is so kind and merciful, so patient, short on anger but long on mercy. His goodness is universal, no exceptions, everything that is comes under his loving care. So everything that is thanks you, O God, your holy ones bless you. They will testify to the glory of your reign, spreading the glad tidings far and wide so that all the world hears of the majesty and splendor of heaven.

Yours is the everlasting realm; yours is the immortal reign. God supports the tottering, and raises those broken by life. Pleading eyes are raised to you, O Lord, and their prayers don't go unanswered. With divine liberality you respond to every need.

Everything God does is perfect, he's kindness itself. He walks by the side of the needy, the ones who know what to ask for. The truly reverent touch his heart, and he's quick to respond to their entreaties. Indeed, his eye is always on his friends, but the devious and crafty— wiped out like *that*.

With mouth and tongue I'll praise God, the human family will bless his name forever, everything that is will glorify him without end.

PRAISE GOD, PRAISE HIM, MY SOUL. Almighty God—I'll spend the rest of my life praising him, I'll praise him as long as there's breath in my body.

Listen to me, friends, don't place any trust in the powerful of this world; they can't save your soul. When they breathe their last, the grave swallows them and all their grand schemes come to nothing. But those who're under God's guidance—what a blessing. They can hope for anything from him. The mighty Lord, Creator of heaven and earth, of the oceans with their incredible array of creatures, he's always true to his word, ever on the side of the victimized and hungry. Those unjustly imprisoned have him as their advocate; the blind see, the depressed are heartened, and the good are encouraged to do better. He takes the alien under his protection, widows and orphans don't ever have to feel abandoned. As for the wicked—fierce retribution.

Listen to me, Zion, God's reign will never end; he'll be your God for all generations.

Hallelujah!

HALLELUJAH!
How wonderful it is to sing God's praises, so soul satisfying, so
fitting. Look at what he's doing; Jerusalem's rising from the dust, her
exiles pouring back into the city, their sorrows over, their wounds
healed, their tears dried.

This God of ours—who's numbered all the stars in heaven and has
a name for each one—how great he is, how powerful, how all-seeing
and wise, how endless his wisdom. See how tender he is with the poor
and needy, but the wicked—he tramples them underfoot.

Sing! Sing out your joy and thanksgiving, strum your guitars, celebrate the God who prepares a vast store of rain-laden clouds in the
sky to water the earth, covering the mountainsides with lush grasses,
giving more than enough grain for humans and cattle alike, and meat
for the cawing crows foraging for their little ones.

The strength of the stallion adds nothing to his joy, nor the skills
of nimble-footed humans. What pleases him is a reverent spirit, a
heart full of the hopeful expectation of his mercy.

Give glory to God, Jerusalem, praise your God, O Zion! He's rein-
forced your city gates and tripled your population; peace reigns
within your borders and your fields rustle with golden grain. His
commands encircle the earth with the speed of light. His snowfalls
are thick as blankets, the white frost covers the walls, icy sleet falls
like crumbs swept from a table. Who can stand the cold? But one
word from him and frozen wastes thaw, warm winds turn icebound
streams into rushing torrents.

This is how God reveals himself to Jacob, his statutes and ordi-
nances to Israel. No other nation can make such a claim, no other
people knows his mind.

Hallelujah!

psalm 148

HALLELUJAH!
Bless God, you heavens, let your farthest reaches ring with praise. Praise God, angels, bless him heavenly armies. You sun and moon praise him, and you bright stars beam your joyful praises. You highest heavens, praise God, and you, too, brimming reservoirs of heaven. All of you join voices in praising God's name. With one word he brought you into being and decreed you'll never pass away.

Earth, join in the exultant praises. All you sea creatures and ocean deeps, bless God. You elements, fire, hail, snow, mist, howling winds—instruments of his will—bless your Creator, come on, mountains and hills, fruit trees and towering cedars, beasts of all kinds, creeping things and flying things, praise the God who made you.

Rulers and all peoples of the earth, leaders and all the powerful, young men and women, the old and children—let them all praise God. His name alone is worthy of praise, he alone reigns over heaven and earth. His chosen ones are raised on high, earning ardent praise for his saints, the saints of Israel, this people so near to his heart.

Hallelujah!

HALLELUJAH!
Let's have a new song in honor of our God, gather the people to hear his praises. Rejoice Israel, let Israel rejoice in its maker; be glad, sing, dance, children of Zion. Strum your guitars, beat your drums—God loves you and the poor are radiant with the beauty of the redeemed. Let the saints, his masterpieces, give him joyful praise; even from their beds at night let their songs resound. Let them enter the battle against the forces of evil with a song on their lips and a flaming sword in their hand. For they're to avenge the living God, to punish the wicked and their leaders with them, to lead the evil away in hand and leg irons, every one of them, every ruler and leader. This honor falls to the saints on the day of wrath.

Hallelujah!

HALLELUJAH!
Praise God in his holy temple;
  praise him who reigns on high!
  Praise him in the fullness of his strength;
  praise him for the marvels he has worked!

Praise him with blaring trumpet blasts;
  praise him with strummed guitars and lutes!
  Praise him with tambourines and dancing feet;
  praise him with strings and flutes!
  Clang cymbals in his praise;
  bang away with exultant joy!

Come! Every living, breathing thing,
Give praise to the Lord!

Hallelujah!